WHO VOTES?

RAYMOND E. WOLFINGER AND STEVEN J. ROSENSTONE

NEW HAVEN AND LONDON, YALE UNIVERSITY PRESS, 1980

Designed by Sally Harris
and set in Caledonia type.
Printed in the United States of America.

Library of Congress Cataloging in Publication Data

Wolfinger, Raymond E.
  Who Votes?

  (A Yale fastback)
  Includes bibliographical references and index.
    1. Elections—United States.   2. Voting—United States.
I. Rosenstone, Steven J., joint author II. Title.
JK1967.W64   324.973'092   79-48068
ISBN 0-300-02541-6
ISBN 0-300-02552-1 pbk.

1 2 3 4 5 6 7 8 9 10

For
Nicholas Holm Wolfinger
and
Caroline Roberts Rosenstone

CONTENTS

ACKNOWLEDGMENTS

Christopher H. Achen generously advised us on many aspects of our data analysis. We are grateful also for comments and suggestions from Richard A. Brody, John A. Ferejohn, Malcolm E. Jewell, Sheila K. Johnson, John H. Kessel, David R. Mayhew, Warren E. Miller, Benjamin I. Page, Samuel Popkin, and Edward R. Tufte. Richard A. McIntosh and Laurie Rhodebeck helped with portions of the computer work. The extraordinary problems of processing our data were overcome with the aid of Margaret Baker, Kathy Janes, Frank Maney, and Harvey Weinstein of the Survey Research Center at the University of California, Berkeley. Thomas Reynolds of the Boalt School of Law at Berkeley kindly advised us on legal research and the use of his school's law library.

For preparing the various drafts of the manuscript we appreciate the help of Catherine Winter and Pat Ramirez of the Institute of Governmental Studies, Tony Kenney of the Department of Political Science, and Mary Brunn of the Survey Research Center, all at Berkeley, and of Ruth Muessig of the Department of Political Science at Yale. Our research was supported in part by grants from the Berkeley Academic Senate Committee on Research and by funds made available by the Department of Political Science at Berkeley.

The survey data we used, from both the Current Population Survey conducted by the Bureau of the Census and the National Election Studies of the University of Michigan's Center for Political Studies, were made available by the Inter-University Consortium for Political and Social Research. Neither the original collectors of the data nor the Consortium are responsible for our analyses or interpretations. An earlier version of chapter 4, entitled "The Effect of Registration Laws on Voter Turnout," appeared in the *American Political Science Review* 72 (March 1978), pp. 22–45.

Marian Neal Ash at Yale University Press was generous with her editorial advice and supervised the book's production with patience and skill.

We are also grateful to Barbara and Caroline for reading our many drafts, offering their comments and encouragement, and sacrificing a good part of four summers while we studied and debated the issues addressed in this book.

1: INTRODUCTION

Elections are at the core of the American political system. They are the way we choose government leaders, a source of the government's legitimacy, and a means by which citizens try to influence public policy. And for most Americans, voting is the only form of political participation.

Since the turn of the century, voter turnout in America has lagged far behind the voting rates in other democratic countries. Scholars, journalists, and politicians have expressed concern over the failure of so many Americans to vote. This concern has increased with the decline in voter participation since 1960. While 62.8 percent of the voting-age population participated in the 1960 election, only 55.5 percent in 1972 and 54.4 percent in 1976 went to the polls. This has caused some observers to raise questions about the health of the American political system and others to propose various reforms intended to facilitate voting.[1]

Before one can come to grips with why turnout is low or why it has declined in recent years, it is necessary to explain why people vote. To do this, one cannot avoid considering why there are such pronounced variations in turnout among different sorts of people. Some groups are almost sure to vote, while others are equally certain to stay home. This book describes and explains variations in turnout among different types of people. Our classification of people is limited to demographic characteristics (age, income, place of residence, and so forth) and to some contextual variables (such as voter registration laws) that can be attributed to individuals once we know what state they live in.

One might think that political scientists long ago identified the simple differences between the voting rates of men and women or rich and poor. In fact, research on this topic has not progressed much beyond a few very broad (and sometimes false) propositions; for example, men vote more than women, and rich people vote more than poor people. There has been remarkably little conclusive evidence about the dimensions of such relationships. What is more, there has been virtually no examination of the more fundamental question, what is the true relationship between turnout and any given demographic characteristic? Do poor people vote less because they have less money or because they are less educated? To what extent is the lower turnout of old people caused by the predominance of women among the elderly? If old women vote less, is it because they are living alone or because they are more likely to believe that voting is men's business? To put it more formally, social scientists have been unable to be very precise about either the strength of relationships between specific demographic characteristics and turnout or whether these relationships persist, once other variables are held constant.

The failure to address such fundamental questions is due in large measure to the fact that the survey samples used in almost all research to date have not been large enough to permit the detailed and precise analysis necessary to answer questions such as those we have just raised. This book is based on analysis of survey samples that are nearly fifty times larger than those ordinarily employed in the study of individual political behavior. These studies, conducted by the Bureau of the Census in November 1972 and 1974, are far superior to any other source of data on the demographic correlates of turnout. The major variables from the census surveys are listed in table 1.1.

Because our samples are so big, we can specify the turnout of particular groups far more precisely than has hitherto been possible. Indeed, we can venture to estimate the voting rates of many groups that have gone unanalyzed because there were too few cases for reliable analysis in the typical national sample—for example, old women or Chicanos. Moreover, we can isolate the effect of a given independent variable. We can, for example, see to what extent the fading turnout of the elderly reflects lower in-

Table 1.1. Variables Used from the November 1972 and
November 1974 Current Population Surveys

Education
Income
Occupation
Employment status (employed, unemployed, not in labor force)
Employer (private, government, self)
Age
Sex
Marital status
Race (white, black, other)
Place of residence (metropolitan area, farm, neither)[a]
State of residence[b]
Registered to vote
Voted
Reason given for not registering or voting
Hispanic ethnicity (Chicano, Puerto Rican, Cuban, other)[c]
How long at present address[c]
How long unemployed[c]
Live in a trailer[c]

---

[a] In 1972 only.
[b] Available for all respondents in 1972 and for some in 1974.
[c] In 1974 only.

come or the death of a spouse. Finally, we can determine
whether the effect of a variable is constant across all types of individuals or falls with particular impact on only some. For example,
is the effect on turnout of being without a spouse greatest for old
people?

By examining the effect that demographic characteristics have
on turnout, we can confirm or reject many propositions about
the motivational foundations of voting. We have been able to test
some of the many theories purporting to explain turnout in general and the voting rates of specific groups in particular. We
have found many widely held propositions contradicted by our
data and have found evidence for new formulations. Unfortunately, disproof is often easier than more affirmative conclusions. At times, several general propositions are equally consistent with the same findings.

Our data describe only a pair of consecutive elections. Therefore we cannot ascertain what sorts of people are most responsible for the decline in turnout that has been a notable feature of American civic life over the past decade. More important, our data are limited to demographic items. We have no information from the census surveys about political interest, information, sense of citizen duty, attitudes about issues, political disaffection, party identification, or any other individual perspective on politics. But within the limited compass of our data, the size of our sample permits much more precise description and detailed analysis than have been attained in other studies of turnout.

Data Sources

The Current Population Survey, conducted by the Bureau of the Census, is a monthly survey of a sample of dwelling units. Interviews are conducted in the third week of the month. The survey was initially intended to measure unemployment and is the source of the Bureau of Labor Statistics' monthly announcements on the subject. In each even-numbered year since 1964, the November Current Population Survey has also included questions on registration and turnout.[2]

Several characteristics of this data file make it particularly well suited for analyzing the demographic correlates of turnout. Most obvious is the sheer size of the sample. In 1972, 93,339 people were interviewed. Weighting to achieve a representative sample of the civilian noninstitutional population yields 136,203 cases for analysis (U.S. Bureau of the Census 1975, appendix A, pp. 4-12). Thus many subpopulations that are represented by only a handful of respondents in the usual national survey are in abundance in our sample. For example, in the most widely used source of individual data on voting, the 1972 National Election Study of the University of Michigan Center for Political Studies, there are 25 males over the age of seventy-eight for whom turnout is reported; there are 1,474 in the 1972 Current Population Survey. The Michigan sample includes 116 people under the age of twenty-one, as compared with 6,905 in the census data; Northern blacks who have attended college number 26 in the Michigan sample and 809 in the census data.

The Current Population Survey includes respondents from all fifty states and uses a very large number of sampling units. The 1972 survey was drawn from 461 primary sampling units (PSUs), as compared with 74 PSUs in the Michigan sample (Center for Political Studies 1973, p. xii; U.S. Bureau of the Census 1963, 1973b, 1975). Taken together, these properties of our sample mean that the sampling variability is very small and the resulting population estimates unusually precise, even for such small subgroups as Chicanos or farmers.

The size of the national sample also means that geographic characterizations of our respondents need not be limited to gross regional divisions. Because of the relatively large number of respondents from almost every state, the effects of voter registration laws and other state-level characteristics can be estimated precisely.[3] This has a further benefit. Because state-by-state variations in the ease of registering to vote are related to region, race, and educational levels (see chapter 4) and because these laws have sizable effects on turnout, particularly for less educated people, controlling for registration provisions is necessary if one wants to isolate relationships between demographic variables and turnout. Finally, because of the large number of respondents from each state, we can also estimate the effect on turnout of other contextual variables such as concurrent elections and different political cultures.

For each survey respondent we added to the Bureau of the Census data contextual data on concurrent gubernatorial and senatorial elections, political culture, and state registration provisions in effect in his state during that year. (Our procedures are described in detail in appendixes B and D.) We were able to do this because each respondent's state of residence was identified in our data file for the 1972 Current Population Survey. This was not the case for the 1974 data. The Bureau of the Census refused to release the code identifying each respondent's state, as it had in 1972. Only twelve states were identified in the 1974 data set; the remainder were divided into subregional groupings. The lack of unique state codes for each respondent makes our estimates for the effect of registration laws in 1974 less precise than we would like.[4] This is one of the reasons why we rely mainly on the 1972 data and generally use the 1974 material when a variable is available only in that year. In any event, our findings for 1972 were duplicated in a separate analysis of the 1974 data (Rosenstone, Wolfinger, and McIntosh 1978) with a few exceptions that are noted as they occur.

We deleted noncitizens from the 1972 sample, thus losing 2,444 actual respondents (the weighted N is 3,522). We also excluded from analysis all cases where the respondent did not know if a vote had been cast or where this information was not ascertained by the interviewer. This further reduced the sample by 2,790 actual respondents; the weighted N is 4,099. These modifications bring us to 88,105 actual respondents; the weighted N for 1972 is 128,582. The same procedure gives us a weighted N of 129,801 for 1974. A fuller description of our sample, including a comparison with other data sets, is in appendix A. This appendix also explains the disparity between the proportion of survey respondents who claim they voted and the much lower turnout rate represented by the familiar measure of the number of ballots divided by the total voting-age population. (The latter measure underestimates turnout, and survey reports exaggerate it). The data coding conventions used in estimating the coefficients reported in the following chapters can be found in appendixes B and D.

Explaining Who Votes

In the company of scholars who have applied formal theory to the study of turnout, we find it useful to think in terms of the benefits and costs of voting to the individual. As Anthony Downs wrote, "Every rational man decides to vote just as he makes all other decisions: if the returns outweigh the costs, he votes; if not, he abstains" (1957, p. 260).

What benefits does voting produce for the individual voter? A single ballot is very unlikely to affect an election outcome (Meehl

1977). Moreover, we are persuaded that few people are brought to the polls by the belief that their vote will make the difference between any candidate's victory and defeat. An *instrumental benefit* does motivate many voters, however. What matters is not the calculated effect of their vote on the outcome but the consequences of the act of voting itself on their immediate well-being. The most obvious example is those people who vote because they are paid to do so (Wolfinger 1974, p. 76). In places where political machines intervene with governments on behalf of private citizens, voting is a way to earn a bit of credit with the organization. Machine politicians asked for favors have been known to base their responses on whether the petitioner voted in the last election (Whyte 1955, p. 194). Members of some private groups that seek political influence may feel that it is prudent to vote. We have no systematic evidence concerning any of these situations, but we do have data on another class of people who might be moved to vote by similar considerations—public employees in places where patronage is important in government personnel decisions. As we will see in chapter 5, voting does seem to have instrumental benefits for many such people.

We suspect also that the act of voting sometimes has an instrumental benefit because it resolves interpersonal pressure. Some people in social environments where a norm of civic duty is strongly manifested might vote in order to avoid being considered deviant. By the same token, satisfying a spouse's expectations doubtless accounts for some trips to the polling place that otherwise would not be made. We may seem to be stretching a point by equating keeping one's job in the Chicago Public Works Department with avoiding social or spousal disapproval. But in both of these situations, the act of voting brings benefits (in the form of suffering avoided) from an external source.

The more important benefits of voting, however, are *expressive* rather than instrumental: a feeling that one has done one's duty to society, to a reference group (Democrats, blacks, bankers, liberals, feminists, conservationists, and so forth), and to oneself; or the feeling that one has affirmed one's allegiance to or efficacy in the political system (Riker and Ordeshook 1973, p. 63). We be-

lieve that the first of these benefits is the most common motivation to vote. As we shall see, the evidence is clear that a sense of
civic duty is related to education, a powerful predictor of turnout
(see table 2.2).

Regardless of how firmly a person believes that his vote will
not affect the outcome, the likelihood that he will vote increases
with his interest in the election. By asserting the primacy of expressive motivations, we do not also "imply that the vote decision
should be independent of the citizen's evaluation of the consequences of the election outcome" (Ferejohn and Fiorina 1979, p.
7). The benefits of an expressive act increase as the individual is
emotionally involved in the object of his expression.

Benefits are only one part of the analytic calculation. The
likelihood that an individual will vote is a direct expression not
only of his motivation to vote but also of the *costs* associated with
doing so. The easier it is for a person to cast a ballot, the more
likely he is to vote. But first he must register, learn something
about the candidates and parties, decide how to vote, and get to
the polls on election day. These are not costless acts; at the very
least they require forfeiting or postponing the opportunity to do
something else that might be more pleasurable. The higher the
cost, the lower the probability of voting. If one must register at
least a month before election day, then voting is costlier than if
one could wait until the last minute, when information about the
election is cheaper because campaign publicity has reached its
peak. By the same token, information is cheaper in presidential
campaigns than in midterm years, thus turnout is higher.

The costs of voting do not fall equally on all segments of the
population. People with political *resources* can more easily bear
the cost of voting. For example, someone experienced in clerical
procedures can more easily overcome the bureaucratic requirements of registering and voting. People who are less adept with
paperwork may find the tasks of registering and voting more
difficult than seems justified by the benefits of voting. For the
most part, of course, the people who can most easily bear the cost
are also those most likely to experience benefits from voting.
The individual demographic characteristics from which we de-

duce motivation are also those that seem most related to the capacity to bear the costs of voting.

A variety of personal characteristics have been suggested as resources, including money, time, social status, experience, information, social contacts, and jobs that put one in contact with government officials (Dahl 1961, p. 226). We cannot measure all resources directly; instead, we infer them from the individual's demographic characteristics. The existing research on this subject does not discriminate between the effects of different resources on voter turnout. This is because instead of analyzing resources separately, existing studies lump them together as a single variable (Downs 1957; Verba and Nie 1972; Verba, Nie, and Kim 1978). Remarkably little effort has been devoted to explaining why certain resources matter and others do not and how much a given resource affects the turnout rates of different sorts of people. A prerequisite to understanding why people vote is determining which of their personal characteristics are most highly related to voting. For example, if experience in dealing with complexity is the most important predictor of turnout, our findings will differ from those in cases where the critical resource is income. What is more, evaluations of proposals for increasing participation depend on which resources are the critical ones. Holding elections on Sundays rather than on Tuesdays will increase turnout only if free time is an important resource, and doing so will have no effect if it is not.

One final consideration bears on our analysis of the benefits, costs, and resources of voting. Nearly all existing research on turnout has assumed, in both the substantive theory and the statistical models employed, that the effect of a particular variable is the same for all types of people. This is probably not true. We believe that although benefits, costs, and resources may accumulate, they may accumulate in a nonadditive way: their marginal effect on the probability of voting is probably not constant across individuals. For those people who are almost certain *not* to vote, the marginal effect of a variable is likely to be very small. As the probability of voting increases, the marginal effect on turnout of additional benefits, costs, or resources also begins to increase.

That is, it takes much more to affect the turnout of someone who is almost certain not to vote than to affect the turnout of someone who is fairly likely to vote. But there is also a second threshold. When a person is more than 50 percent likely to vote, the effect of additional benefits, costs or resources on the probability of voting begins to decrease. Thus someone who is almost certain to vote, like the person who is almost certain *not* to vote, is probably relatively unaffected by small changes in the benefits, costs, or resources of participation. For example, as people go from youth into middle age, they are more likely to vote. But the relationship between age and turnout may be much stronger for people with little education than for college graduates who are likely to vote even when young. We believe that the presence of such relationships gives rise to empirical questions that should not be foreclosed by a priori assumptions; we have analyzed our data accordingly.

As Downs acknowledged, any human activity can be explained in terms of costs and benefits. Like other formulations that in principle explain everything, cost-benefits calculations run the risk of explaining nothing (Barry 1970, p. 43n). This is particularly true when all manner of intangible and emotional benefits and costs are included. We hope to avoid this pitfall by concentrating on differences among the turnout rates of different types of individuals rather than trying to explain why anyone bothers to vote. Our data permit us to discriminate among a variety of factors that affect the likelihood of voting.

Estimating the Effect of Demographic and Contextual Variables on the Probability of Voting

The benefits and costs of voting vary among individuals. Education, occupation, income, age, and marital status are commonly thought to be related to the likelihood of voting. These variables are also correlated with each other. Professionals are likely to have more education and money than do blue-collar workers. On average, the elderly have much less formal education than the young, but their incomes are far more comparable. The intercorrelations among these variables mean that a researcher wishing to isolate the effect on voting of a single variable must control for each of the individual's other characteristics. For the same reasons, the restrictiveness of the registration laws must also be held constant. It is impossible to use cross-tabulations for this purpose because too many relationships have to be taken into account. The complex interrelatedness of the variables requires a multivariate technique to produce estimates that are statistically consistent and efficient.

Probably the most common procedure for doing this is ordinary least squares (OLS) regression. But our data do not meet the usual OLS assumptions because our dependent variable, turnout, is dichotomous. Therefore we used probit analysis to estimate the effect of the variables. (See appendix C for a comparison of probit and OLS.) Like OLS, probit allows us to estimate the marginal effect of a single independent variable on the dependent variable while holding constant all other independent variables in the equation.

Probit has another major advantage. As a statistical model, it is a more faithful representation of our substantive theory than is OLS. As we will see, the impact of most demographic variables on the probability of voting is not constant across all types of individuals. Rather, the effect of a variable depends on the probability that the individual would vote. For example, a high-status occupation or a high income has less impact on a college graduate, who is 90 percent likely to vote, than it has on a high school dropout, who is only 55 percent likely to vote. The probit model takes this into account. With OLS a variable has the same impact on all types of people. With probit a variable has very little impact on those who are either very unlikely or nearly certain to vote. It has the greatest impact in the middle of the distribution, on those who are between 40 and 60 percent likely to vote and are most susceptible to the forces pushing them to vote or not to vote. For example, let us suppose that an individual characteristic (represented by a dummy variable) has a probit coefficient of .20. For those who are either 10 percent likely to vote or 90 percent likely to vote, the probability of voting would increase by approximately 3 percent as a result of being scored "one" on this variable. Among those who are between 40 percent and 60 percent likely to vote, the probability of voting would increase by approximately 8 percent.

Because of the tremendous cost of estimating a series of equations using all the respondents in our sample, we took a subsample for the probit analysis.[5] We ignored the sample weight and randomly selected 10 percent of the actual respondents. The resulting subsample of 8,334 actual respondents was used in making the probit estimates of the partial effect of each variable.[6] In no way do we bias our estimates by using this subsample instead of the full sample. The only statistical "cost" is a slight increase in the standard error of each estimate.[7] Even after taking the subsample, we are still left with an ample number of cases in the many subpopulations that we will be analyzing; for example, 72 men over the age of seventy-eight, 656 people under the age of twenty-one, and 73 Northern blacks who have attended college.[8]

The probit estimates are reported in equation 1 (in appendix C). The variables in this equation are education, income, occupation, race, age, region, sex, marital status, inability to work, size of place of residence, whether one is a government employee, and a set of variables describing the type of state in which the respondent lives—its registration laws, whether there was a gubernatorial election in 1972, and the political culture. Each of the variables that was deleted from this equation as a result of the preliminary analysis affected the probability of voting by less than 1 percent. These coefficients are reported at the appropriate places in the text.[9]

In the chapters that follow, two statistics are reported. The first is the simple percentage of the respondents with a given demographic characteristic who voted. This is based upon cross-tabulations using the full sample (weighted N of 128,582). This percentage is provided for descriptive purposes only. The second statistic is the estimate of the marginal effect on the probability of voting of the variables in the equation. These estimates are derived from equation 1 in appendix C. The second set of statistics—the estimated partial impact of each variable—will be the main object of our attention.

2: *SORTING OUT THE EFFECTS OF SOCIOECONOMIC STATUS*

Probably the best-known finding about turnout is that "citizens of higher social and economic status participate more in politics. This generalization . . . holds true whether one uses level of education, income, or occupation as the measure of social status" (Verba and Nie 1972, p. 125). This statement is as well documented as it is familiar. College graduates vote more than high school graduates; white-collar workers vote more than blue-collar workers; and the rich vote more than the poor.

These three demographic characteristics are related to each other. People with more schooling have better jobs and make more money and so on. But the interrelationships are far from perfect. The vast majority of Americans with only grade-school educations had family incomes under $10,000 in 1972, but so did half the people whose education stopped with high school, and so did a quarter of all college graduates. One can easily think of occupations where the educational and income levels seem inconsistent or mismatched, for example, librarians and plumbers.

Because there are so many people whose education, occupations, and incomes are "inconsistent," it is possible to explore the obvious question: what is the relationship to turnout of *each* of these attributes? Do rich people vote more because they have better jobs and more schooling or just because they have more money? Does the high turnout of college graduates reflect their education, their better jobs, or their higher salaries? Or is each of these characteristics related to turnout? Do certain combinations of attributes, for example, high education and low income, produce distinctive patterns of voting? Do the people in some occupations vote more than would otherwise be expected?

Answers to such questions are important for several reasons. In the first place, different theories of why people vote emphasize the explanatory power of one or another of the components of socioeconomic status (SES). Information costs, for example, are primarily related to education. More schooling creates greater ability to learn about politics without anxiety and to master the bureaucratic aspects of registering and voting. On the other hand, an immediate social environment that valued civic participation might be more related to one's occupation. We will discuss specific causal propositions in detail when we consider each individual variable. Here we need only point out that establishing the relative importance of each component of SES helps us assess many generalizations about why some people vote more than others.

In the second place, sorting out the individual importance of education, jobs, and income as independent variables will allow us later to analyze properly the effect of other demographic characteristics such as race, age, and sex. These attributes are unevenly related to both the components of status and to turnout. For example, it is well known that turnout increases with age. And it is obvious (although usually not acknowledged) that income reaches its peak in middle age, while almost everyone is finished with school by age twenty-five. Although income increases with age at any given educational level, the rate of increase is not comparable across all levels of education. The association between income and age, although positive, is rather modest for people with less education and becomes progressively stronger for the better educated. The proportion of high school graduates with family incomes over $15,000 is only 50 percent greater for those aged thirty-seven to sixty-nine than it is for the youngest adults. For people with postgraduate education, on the other hand, the increase is fully 200 percent. These findings are displayed in table 2.1, which shows another facet of the same point: the relationship between income and education is relatively slight among the young and becomes stronger with age. It also appears that people in some educational categories experi-

Table 2.1. Relationship between Education and Income,
by Age, in 1972

*Percent with family incomes of
$15,000 or more*

Age	High school graduates	Some college	College graduates	5+ years of college
18–24	16	28	24	22
25–31	12	22	34	40
32–36	18	31	49	57
37–69	24	38	55	67
70+	8	10	17	23
Total	19	30	43	54

ence a temporary decline in earnings after their early twenties, perhaps because wives leave the labor market to become mothers.

These findings suggest the possibility that part of the relationship between income and turnout reported in previous studies reflects the greater age of people with more money, and so the low turnout of the young might result only from their modest incomes. Our huge sample allows us to test these speculations easily by holding age and other demographic variables constant as we analyze the effect of each variable on turnout.

As we have seen, the components of SES are separable both theoretically and empirically. One way to analyze their relationship to turnout is illustrated by this description of the creation of an omnibus SES variable:

> The index of family social and economic status was based upon the respondents' education, family income and occupation of head of household. Each of the variables were [*sic*] standardized and then summed, creating a simple additive index with equal weight given to education, income, and occupation. If occupation was unobtainable, it was estimated on the basis of income and education. . . . We divide the "SES" scale into sixths. The relationship between socioeconomic status and overall participation is linear and fairly strong. [Verba and Nie 1972, pp. 366, 130]

A similar approach was also employed in Verba, Nie, and Kim (1978). Combining variables this way disguises the individual effect of each variable. We will see that the assumptions implicit in the procedure used by Verba and Nie are wrong: (1) the three components are not equally related to turnout, (2) their effect is not additive, and (3) the relationships are often not linear. We will therefore treat education, income, and occupation not as measures of a broader, inclusive characteristic called "socioeconomic status" but as three separate variables measuring distinct attributes.

Some researchers have described the influence on turnout of each of the three variables, thus avoiding the pitfall of treating SES as an omnibus variable rather than simply as a useful generic label. Unfortunately, the size of conventional survey samples does not permit the use of very discriminating categories. A good illustration is the analysis by Bennett and Klecka of the combined samples from three Michigan election studies, in which each SES component was measured by "high," "medium," and "low" categories. Their warning that this procedure might blur important distinctions and produce "misrepresentations of the results" (Bennett and Klecka 1970, p. 366n) is justified by our findings from the census sample. For example, professionals are generally combined with managers and administrators to form the upper middle class, which comprises about a quarter of the labor force. This is consistent with the similar income distributions in these two occupational categories. The problem is that the professionals are far better educated: 80 percent have attended college, as compared with 45 percent of the managers and administrators.

The large Current Population Survey sample permits the use of more refined descriptive categories. Our brief discussion of research performed without this advantage is intended both to explain our research strategy and to suggest reasons why our findings sometimes differ from those of other researchers. We begin by describing the voting rate of people with different educations, incomes, and occupations.

Bivariate Relationships to Turnout

Education has usually been found to be the demographic variable most strongly related to turnout (Campbell et al. 1960, pp. 476–78; Milbrath 1965, pp. 122–23; Barber 1969, pp. 11–14). Some researchers, however, report that it is less important than income (Bennett and Klecka 1970; Verba, Nie, and Kim 1978). Milbrath and Goel (1977, p. 102) conclude from their survey of the literature that education has no "consistent impact on voting."

We have found a very strong relationship between rates of voting and years of education, as shown in figure 2.1. Only 38 percent of respondents with fewer than five years of school went to the polls, as compared with 69 percent of those who stopped

Figure 2.1. Education and Turnout in 1972

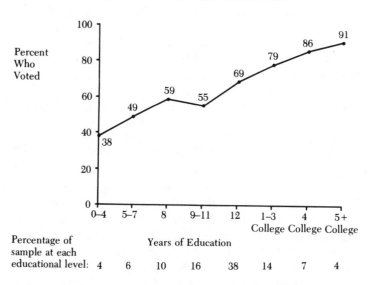

with a high school diploma, 86 percent of college graduates, and 91 percent of people with at least a year of graduate school.

When we classify people by the length of their formal education, we are measuring several different attributes. American schools provide a good deal of explicit instruction and exhortation on citizenship that emphasizes the obligation to vote and thus might be thought to nurture a sense of citizen duty. The better educated are more likely to know social norms (Sniderman 1975). Our analysis of data from the Michigan 1972 National Election Study shows that about 60 percent of college graduates express a strong sense of citizen duty, as compared with half the high school graduates and about 40 percent of those with less education (see table 2.2). It seems reasonable, then, to think that education increases the moral pressure to vote.

Perhaps more important, education imparts information about politics and cognate fields and about a variety of skills, some of which facilitate political learning. Reading is the most important and obvious skill. Schooling increases one's capacity for understanding and working with complex, abstract, and intangible subjects, that is, subjects like politics. As table 2.2 shows, educated people are more likely to be well informed about politics and to follow the campaign in the mass media. Learning about politics doubtless heightens interest; the more sense one can make of the political world, the more likely one is to pay attention to it. If we assume that incomprehension produces anxiety and avoidance, then anything that increases understanding facilitates interest. Furthermore, education increases one's ability to handle the humdrum bureaucratic requirements of registering and voting. A better educated person is more likely to know about such matters or to be able to find out easily. In a number of respects, then, education cuts the costs of the voting decision and of the act of voting. At the same time, educated people are more likely to be involved in the issues or in the intrinsic value of voting and thus are more likely to be emotionally gratified by going to the polls.

It is difficult to determine to what extent these skills and interests are a consequence of going through the school system and to

Table 2.2. Relationship between Education and Civic Virtue in 1972

Years of education	% Who express a high sense of citizen duty [a]	% Who say they are very interested in politics	% Who use the mass media at a high rate [b]	% Who are well informed about politics [c]
0–4	42	16	11	5
5–7	41	22	26	8
8	44	27	33	17
9–11	39	28	31	14
12	50	34	35	17
1–3 college	52	47	53	32
4 college	56	55	68	37
5+ college	66	75	68	59

Source: Authors' analysis of data from Center for Political Studies 1972 National Election Study.

[a] Respondents who disagreed with these statements: "It isn't so important to vote when you know your party doesn't have a chance to win." "So many people vote in the national election that it doesn't matter much to me whether I vote or not." "If a person doesn't care how an election comes out he shouldn't vote in it." "A good many local elections aren't important enough to bother with."

[b] Respondents who did at least three of the following: read about the campaign in the newspapers; listened to speeches or discussions about the campaign on the radio; read about the campaign in magazines; watched programs about the campaign on television.

[c] Respondents who knew at least five of the following six political facts: the number of terms a president can serve; the length of a term for a U.S. senator; the length of a term for a U.S. representative; the names of the House candidates in his district; the party controlling Congress before the election; the party controlling Congress after the election.

what extent they reflect the personal qualities of the type of person who gets an education. Level of education indicates not only the skills and duties learned in school but characteristics of the individual that are unrelated to school. People who are likely to make it through college are also likely to make it to the polls. In part this is because years of schooling reflect family background more than any other demographic characteristic does. People who have gone to college are more likely to have educated and/or affluent parents. As a result, they are more likely to come from homes where books, newspapers, and magazines were read and where politics was discussed. By virtue of this socialization, those who have been to college have grown up exposed to politics and experienced in dealing with information about it.

Identifying the relationship of education to turnout requires that we isolate the effect of schooling from those of occupation and income, since it is positively related to these variables. Before doing this, however, we will look briefly at the bivariate relationships between voting and income and occupation.

Researchers have consistently found a strong positive relationship between income and turnout (Milbrath and Goel 1977, pp. 97–98), and some report that income has more impact than other variables (Bennett and Klecka 1970). We found that turnout increases with income, as figure 2.2 shows. People earning less than $2,000 a year were 40 percentage points below the turnout of those enjoying family incomes of more than $25,000.

Although the literature abounds with data showing that rich people vote more, very little explanation has been offered beyond the statement that the more money people have, the more likely they are to be educated and thus to bear all the marks of exposure to school (Milbrath and Goel 1977, pp. 97–98). This comment is not very satisfactory, of course, since it provides no reason for thinking that income has any independent explanatory power. We can think of several reasons to expect income in and of itself to be related to turnout:

1. Desperately poor people are preoccupied by the struggle to keep body and soul together. No matter what they learned in school, they have no time or emotional energy for nonessentials such as voting.
2. Irrespective of their educational backgrounds, well-to-do people are likely to acquire in their jobs the interests and skills that lead to political involvement and voting.

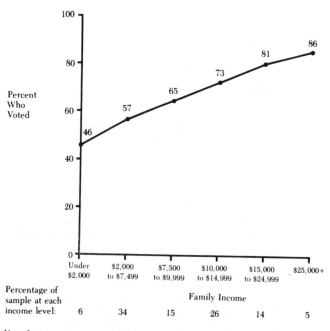

Figure 2.2. Income and Turnout in 1972

Note: Income was not reported for 8,835 cases, which were excluded from these tabulations. Smaller income groupings were collapsed into these categories when there were no consequential differences in their turnout.

3. More than schooling or occupation, income determines one's neighborhood and, perhaps, avocational companions and thus exposure to a variety of norms and pressures. If income is high relative to the other two indices of social status, the consequence will be adult socialization conducive to high turnout. The opposite will result from disproportionately low income.

4. Someone who has succeeded materially despite a scanty education is probably unusually competent, energetic, and engaged. This is all the more true if the person does not have a high-status job. These personal qualities may well generate a keen sense of citizen duty and therefore a high

probability of voting. The same would be true in reverse for someone who could not be successful, despite the advantage of a good education.

5. Rich people have a bigger "stake in the system" and thus are more highly motivated both to make the appropriate choice on election day and to support the political system by participating in it.

We will see how these assorted speculations fare after a look at the voting rates of people in different occupations.

The relationship between occupation and turnout is also well accepted in the literature: the higher the job status, the greater the probability of voting (Lane 1959, p. 49; Lipset 1960, p. 189; Milbrath and Goel 1977, pp. 102–106). We found considerable variation in 1972 among different occupations, as table 2.3 shows. Professional and technical workers (hereafter simply "professionals") had the highest turnout—86 percent—followed by farmers and managers and administrators, 79 percent of whom voted. Seventy-five percent of clerks and salespeople voted. Turnout was considerably lower in blue-collar occupations: 64 percent for skilled workers, 63 percent for nondomestic service workers, and 53 percent for unskilled and semiskilled workers. The lowest group by far (as well as the smallest) was farm laborers and foremen, of whom only 46 percent went to the polls.

In a very general way, these findings are what we might expect. Occupations are related to turnout for many of the same reasons that education is. Some kinds of jobs develop bureaucratic skills or familiarize their incumbents with intangibles. Some positions bring one into contact with subject matter that bears directly on politics or on issues that are the subject of political discussion. Jobs are a prime locus of friendship and interpersonal relations, exposing the individual to norms of appropriate behavior. Nevertheless, some of the figures in table 2.3 are somewhat surprising. We did not expect, for example, to find such high turnout among farmers or so small a gap between the lower-middle-class and upper-middle-class occupations.

Table 2.3.   Occupations and Turnout in 1972

Occupation of respondent	Percent of labor force	Percent who voted
Upper middle class:		
Professional and technical	15%	86
Managers and administrators	10	79
Lower middle class:		
Clerks and salespeople	24	75
Working class:		
Skilled workers	13	64
Semiskilled and unskilled workers	23	53
Nondomestic service workers	11	63
Agriculture:		
Farmers and farm managers	2	79
Farm laborers and foremen	1	46
Total	99%	—

Note: Excluded from this table and all calculations involving occupation are 49,162 cases not in the labor force and 261 cases without previous full-time work experience.

Isolating the Effect of Education and Income on Turnout

The findings in the preceding section are useful chiefly as a prologue to more detailed analysis. Because education, income, and occupation are so interrelated, we cannot identify the relationship of any one of them to turnout unless we hold constant the effect of the other two, as well as that of other variables such as age. Doing this confirms the very strong effect of education and shows that the effect of income is modest and limited. These findings set the stage for analysis of the more complex and interesting variations in turnout among people in different occupations.

Using equation 1, we examine the relationship between education and turnout, with all other variables held constant.[1] Table 2.4 presents, for each income category, the effect on turnout of increases in education, using as a base point respondents with

Table 2.4.   Effect of Education
on Turnout, by Income (in Percent)

			Years of education				
					College		
Income	*5–7*	*8*	*9–11*	*12*	*1–3*	*4*	*5+*
Under $2,000	4	8	13	21	32	42	55
$2,000–$7,499	4	8	14	22	32	41	50
$7,500–$9,999	4	8	14	22	32	41	46
$10,000–$14,999	4	8	14	22	31	39	41
$15,000–$24,999	4	8	14	21	30	36	38
$25,000+	3	8	14	21	29	34	33
Total	4	8	14	22	31	38	40

Note: The number in each cell is the probit estimate (see appendix C) of the increase in percentage turnout over the turnout for the lowest education category. For example, people earning less than $2,000 with twelve years of schooling would have a voting rate 21 percentage points higher than people in the same income category who had fewer than five years of schooling.

fewer than five years of schooling. It shows that even after controlling for all other variables, education has a very powerful independent effect on the likelihood of voting. For example, among people earning $10,000 to $14,999, high school graduates were 22 percent likelier to vote than their counterparts with fewer than five years of schooling. The increase for people at the same income level with postgraduate training was 41 percentage points.

At every level of income, increases in education raise the probability that a person will go to the polls. Increases in education through high school graduation have the same effect in all income categories. Finishing grammar school raises turnout by 8 percent, irrespective of income. Getting a high school diploma increases the probability of voting by 22 percent across the board.

The effect of a college education, however, varies inversely with income. Going to college has the most impact on the poorest people and somewhat less on those in the higher income brackets. A college degree produces a 42 percent increase in turnout for people earning less than $2,000. This is an exotic combination, and we are unsure what kinds of people populate the category. As income rises, the effect of college attendance diminishes somewhat, to the point where it increases turnout by "only" 34 percent for those earning more than $25,000.

Roughly the same pattern holds if we substitute occupation for income in this analysis: education has the greatest effect on the probability that those in the lowest status categories will vote. Even here, however, the differences are very large. By any standards, education has a powerful independent influence on turnout.

The same cannot be said for income. Table 2.5, the obverse of table 2.4, shows the independent effect of income on turnout for people at different levels of education.[2] When other variables are controlled, income is still related to turnout, but its effect is relatively small. Our first conclusion, then, is that income has much less effect on turnout than does education. Second, income has the greatest effect on people who have not graduated from college. For anyone without a degree, an income of $7,500 to $9,999 increases the probability of voting about 13 percentage points above the rate of the poorest respondents. The corresponding increase for college graduates is 10 percent, and for people with graduate training it is only 7 percent. The third conclusion is based on our finding that additional income beyond $10,000 does not affect the turnout of people who have been to college and that increases past $15,000 do not substantially increase the probability that people with less education will vote. We conclude that income affects turnout only to the point where a modestly comfortable standard of living has been attained. Once this threshold has been reached, more money has no effect on the likelihood of voting. Analyzing the marginal effect of income on different occupational groups produces a similar result: beyond the middle income categories, higher income does not

Table 2.5.   Effect of Income
on Turnout, by Education (in Percent)

Years of education	Family income				
	$2,000–$7,499	$7,500–$9,999	$10,000–$14,999	$15,000–$24,999	$25,000+
0–8 (grammar school)	7	13	15	17	18
9–12 (high school)	8	13	15	16	18
1–3 college	7	13	14	15	16
4 college	6	10	11	11	11
5+ college	4	7	6	6	5
Total	7	13	14	14	14

Note: The format is the same as in table 2.4. The number in each cell is the probit estimate (see appendix C) of the increase in percentage turnout over the turnout of people in the lowest income category, those earning less than $2,000. For example, college graduates with incomes of more than $25,000 have a turnout rate 11 percentage points higher than college graduates with family incomes below $2,000.

increase turnout. The effect of income on turnout is about the same for all occupations.

These findings lend some support to the first of our five speculations about the effect of income on turnout: rock-bottom poverty seems to depress turnout somewhat. Beyond that, income does not have much effect on turnout. Above the poverty level, once we know a person's educational attainment, our ability to predict whether he will vote is not substantially improved by knowing how much money he makes. Thus we can reject those hypotheses that attribute turnout to high income.

Voting Rates of Different Occupations

In one sense, our findings about turnout by different occupations resemble those for income: once education is controlled, variations from one type of job to the next become rather modest, as table 2.6 shows. But some interesting and unexpected patterns in these relationships bear on several general propositions about turnout.

Table 2.6.   Effect of Occupation
on Turnout, by Education (in Percent)

| Years of education | Occupation | | | | | |
	Profes- sionals	Man- agers	Farm owners	Clerical and sales	Service workers	Farm laborers
0–8 (grammar school)	8	3	18	13	6	−5
9–12 (high school)	7	3	16	12	6	−6
1–3 college	7	3	13	11	5	−6
4 college	5	2	9	8	4	−6
5+ college	2	1	a	5	2	a
Total	5	3	16	11	6	−5

Note: The format is the same as in table 2.4. The number in each cell is the probit estimate (see appendix C) of the increase (or decrease, in the case of farm laborers) in turnout over the turnout of skilled, semiskilled, and unskilled workers. For example, farm owners who have attended high school have a voting rate 16 percentage points higher than that of blue-collar workers with similar education.

[a] Too few cases for a reliable estimate.

The broadest generalization suggested by table 2.6 is that the effect of occupation is greatest for the least educated and dwindles almost to nothing for college graduates.[3] The impact of any occupational category on the probability of voting is two to three times greater for people with a grammar-school education than for those with at least a year of graduate work. This suggests that some job experiences have consequences on turnout similar to those of education. Uneducated people, it seems, learn from certain kinds of jobs the skills and norms imparted in school.

Since people at the top of the occupational status ladder vote the most, it is generally thought that their jobs involve certain kinds of stimuli that are particularly conducive to political participation (Milbrath and Goel 1977, p. 103). One thought is that their superordinate work relationships give them a sense of mastery that is generalized to high feelings of political efficacy. Another argument is that their work leads to contact with officials or at least to talk about politics. It is also believed that members of the upper middle class have more time to spend reading about and participating in politics and thus can more easily bear the costs of the mechanical aspects of voting.

Our data, however, show that upper-middle-class occupations are not strongly related to turnout. When other demographic variables are controlled, the marginal effect of being a professional is small and that of being a manager is almost nonexistent. The only consequential impact is among professionals without postgraduate training, and even here the increment is only 5 to 8 percent. More important, the effect of these high-status occupations is smaller than that of a clerical or sales job. With other variables controlled, managers are between 4 and 10 percent less likely to vote than are members of the lower middle class with the same education, and professionals are between 3 and 5 percent less likely to vote. Our multivariate analysis shows that these lower status white-collar jobs in fact have a much greater marginal effect on voting. Clerks and salespeople with a grammar-school education are 13 percent more likely to vote than are comparable blue-collar workers. Those with a college degree are 8 percent likelier to vote.

Our findings about the effect of occupation and income are inconsistent with theories of voting that posit money or time as resources facilitating turnout (Milbrath 1965, p. 135; Frey 1971, pp. 101–05; Frey 1972, pp. 119–22; Milbrath and Goel 1977, p. 103). We saw in table 2.5 that people in the highest income groups were no more likely to vote than were people with middle incomes. By itself, wealth does not increase one's probability of voting beyond what would be expected for someone of moderate income.

By the same token, there is no support for the argument that people with higher status vote more because they have more free time for nonessentials like talking about politics, registering, and voting. Two different time-use studies show that blue-collar workers have as much free time, both formal and informal, as do white-collar workers (Robinson and Converse 1972, pp. 74–75;

Strafford and Duncan 1977, table 8). It will not do to say that the important thing is not the amount of free time but one's ability to control it, for clerks and salespeople surely have no more autonomy in this respect than do members of the working class. Farmers probably work longer hours than any other occupational group does, but they also have exceptionally high rates of turnout. Finally, if free time had anything to do with voting, we would expect to see its effect in differences between employed and unemployed women. Working women have much less free time than housewives do (Robinson and Converse 1972, pp. 74–75), yet as we shall see in chapter 3, these two groups have virtually identical rates of turnout.

For the final piece of evidence that free time does not lead to higher turnout, we might consider those people with the most time on their hands—the unemployed. Compared to people working full time, the unemployed are 1 to 3 percent less likely to vote.[4] Moreover, those who are classified as unable to work are also unlikely to vote.

In short, free time is not a resource that facilitates voting.

These findings help us identify the elements of middle-class job experiences that lead to higher turnout. Compared to manual workers, all people in white-collar jobs have this in common: they deal with abstractions and intangibles, that is, with paperwork. Their jobs require verbal and communications skills not usually demanded of blue-collar workers. The subject matter of politics is also intangible for most people, hence any kind of middle-class job, no matter how humble, helps one deal with political information.

Another characteristic that many clerks and salespeople have in common with most professionals and managers is subjective identification with the middle class. Forty-six percent of these lower white-collar workers in the 1972 Michigan survey said that they considered themselves members of the middle class, as compared with less than 30 percent of blue-collar workers. We think it possible that people in sales and clerical jobs who differentiate themselves from the working class and identify with the middle class might well be more likely to adopt what they consider the appropriate habits. If voting is thought to be a characteristic of the more socially elevated elements in society, perhaps people aspiring to middle-class identity would be more likely to vote.

The Rural and Agricultural Sectors

Understanding of farmers' voting habits is clouded by imprecision about definitions and, in particular, a tendency to talk interchangeably about farmers and about people who don't live in cities. Milbrath and Goel, for example, say that "farmers are less likely to become active in politics than [are] city dwellers" (1977, p. 106). *But most people who are not city dwellers do not live on farms.* More than 70 percent of all our respondents live in Standard Metropolitan Statistical Areas (SMSAs). Only about one in seven of the rural residents lives on a farm. There is considerable controversy about whether people who live in the country are less likely to vote than city residents (Lane 1959, pp. 49–50; Nie, Powell, and Prewitt 1969, p. 368; Verba and Nie 1972, pp. 237–38, 243; Milbrath and Goel 1977, pp. 106–10). Controlling for the variables in equation 1, we found no difference in turnout between people who live on farms and those who live in SMSAs. (The probit estimate is −.034 and the standard error is .082.) Nonmetropolitan residents who did not live on farms were 1 to 3 percent less likely to vote than were either of the other two groups. These findings lead us to think that there are limits to theories of turnout that emphasize "center-periphery" differences (Verba and Nie 1972, chapter 13; Milbrath and Goel 1977, chapter 4).[5]

Before we consider farmers' voting rates, a further distinction is necessary. Living on a farm and being a farmer are not the same thing; in fact, most people who live on farms are not farmers. We classify as farmers those people whose principal occupation is farm owner or farm manager, and we put farm laborers and foremen in a separate group labeled "farm workers."

"Farmer" is an occupational category; it does not refer to one's place of residence.[6] Although 82 percent of farmers live on farms, most of the people who make their homes on farms do not also make their living there. Only 34 percent of the labor force who lived on farms in 1972 were farmers; another 14 percent were farm workers, and the rest pursued a variety of other occupations. Farmers have considerably less schooling and income than other farm residents do. For example, in 1972 14 percent of farmers had attended college, as compared with 31 percent of other members of the labor force who lived on farms.

With these preliminaries out of the way, we can more fruitfully describe the extraordinarily high turnout of farmers. In 1972, farmers voted more than every other occupational group except professionals. In 1974 they had the highest turnout rate of any group: 66 percent, as compared with 64 percent for professionals and 62 percent for managers and administrators. This contrasts with the portrait of agrarian apathy in the 1950s that was presented in *The American Voter* (Campbell et al. 1960, chapter 15).[7] Michael Lewis-Beck's 1977 study shows that farm turnout rose substantially in the intervening years. In the same period the farm population diminished by about two-thirds and became better educated and more prosperous. Lewis-Beck attributes the increase in turnout to farmers' economic gains.[8] But farmers still trail virtually all occupation groups in income. In 1972, 11 percent of farmers earned more than $15,000, as compared with 42 percent of professionals and 41 percent of managers. The gap in education is even greater.

Controlling for income, age, education, and other demographic variables increases the difference in turnout between farmers and everyone else, as table 2.6 shows. If we hold these and other variables constant, farmers' turnout in 1972 was 16 percent higher than would otherwise be expected. The corresponding estimate for 1974 is a bit lower, but for that year we were able to control for the length of time each resident had lived at his present address. Because farmers move less often than everyone else, adding this variable to the analysis reduces somewhat the effect of being a farmer. (Sixty-nine percent of farmers had not moved in the previous ten years, as compared with 37 percent of the rest of the population.) In short, farmers' remarkably high voting rates cannot be explained by their other demographic characteristics.

Farmers work for themselves and therefore bear the ultimate responsibility for what they do. They must deal in their own interests with buyers, suppliers, and employees. Such a high level of self-reliance and so many clerical relationships might teach the skills that help one understand politics and might heighten awareness of relationships between government and the self. Moreover, people able to function so on their own might have more of the personal qualities that we associate with political involvement. If this line of argument is valid, it should apply not just to farmers but to all the self-employed. We tested this proposition by including a dummy variable for self-employment in equation 1. This variable had no significant effect. (The probit estimate was .062, with a standard error of .083.) The coefficient was also near zero when we tested the proposition that self-employment was related to turnout only for people who had not attended college. (The probit estimate was .054, with a standard error of .098.) Plausible as the self-employment explanation may be, we can find no empirical support for it in our data and must look elsewhere to understand the high level of farm voting.

We think that the explanation for farmers' exceptional turnout lies in two other aspects of their lives. One is the variety of their relations with government. Innumerable public programs give and loan money, limit production, buy crops, guarantee prices, regulate farm labor, give advice, improve land, provide water, and so on. These services are most important to farmers who grow cash crops, the part of agriculture that has overshadowed the old-fashioned subsistence farming. Federal, state, and county officials are in constant contact with farmers about hundreds of subjects. Many agricultural programs are administered by committees of farmers. All of these interactions with government develop the bureaucratic skill that is otherwise a product of conventional education and heighten farmers' sense of the personal relevance of politics.

A second factor that contributes to farmers' political awareness is the wide fluctuations in their economic fortunes, often because of real or imagined government actions. Harvests have a climactic, all-or-nothing quality, and agricultural commodity markets are notoriously volatile. Unlike people whose periods of greater and lesser prosperity are relatively moderate, many farmers regularly experience a boom or a bust. For example, the net income of farm operators rose from $18,665 million in 1972 to $33,349 million in 1973, and fell to $26,130 million the following year. Between 1970 and 1976 the price of a bushel of wheat ranged from $1.33 to $4.09. The cost of seeds to farmers went from $927 million in 1970 to $2,082 million in 1974. Government payments to farmers, which amounted to $3,961 million in 1972, fell to $531 million two years later. The export market for farm commodities fluctuated from 14 percent in 1971 to 21 percent in 1973 (U.S. Bureau of the Census 1977, section 24).

More than most people, farmers observe governmental actions whose impact on their prosperity is direct and easily understood. There is nothing esoteric or abstract about an embargo on wheat sales to the Soviet Union or the termination of a price support program. The perpetual uncertainty about harvests and markets, combined with governmental involvement in many aspects of farming, raises farmers' political consciousness to a level attained by few other groups.

The higher relative turnout of farmers in 1974 is the first point in our analysis where the availability of data for that year leads to any modification of our findings. We will return to differences between midterm and presidential elections in discussing the voting rates of young people. Otherwise, our conclusions about the demographic correlates of turnout in presidential years are equally valid for midterm elections. For detailed comparison of presidential and midterm electorates, see Rosenstone, Wolfinger, and McIntosh (1978).

The agricultural sector also includes the lowest turnout group

—farm workers. Only 46 percent of them reported going to the polls in 1972, well below the figure for nonagricultural manual laborers. Much of their lower turnout can be explained by other demographic variables such as differences in education, income, and region of residence. Even controlling for the variables in equation 1, turnout among farm workers is still about 6 percentage points lower than would otherwise be expected. Some common stereotypes of farm workers that might be thought to explain this gap are wide of the mark. First, contrary to popular political mythology, only 14 percent of farm laborers are Chicanos. Second, farm workers are not more mobile than the rest of the population.[9] Indeed, they move somewhat less than professionals. Moreover, our probit equation for 1974, which included terms both for mobility and ethnicity (and for trailer residence), yielded the same gap of 6 percentage points in farm worker turnout. We have no idea why this should be.

Implications

The disaggregation of the effect of socioeconomic status on turnout reveals that education, income, and occupation have different effects on voter turnout. Education has a very substantial effect on the probability that one will vote. Citizens with a college degree are 38 percent more likely to vote than are people with fewer than five years of schooling. The effect is greatest among those with the least education.

Income, on the other hand, has a much smaller effect on voter turnout. Compared with people in the lowest income category, those with family incomes of $25,000 or more were 14 percent more likely to vote. Income affects turnout only to the point where a modestly comfortable standard of living has been attained. Once this threshold has been reached, more money has no additional impact on the likelihood of voting. The very rich are no more likely to vote than are those with middle incomes.

Finally, the noteworthy variations in the turnout of people in different occupations are not between higher and lower status occupations. The larger and more interesting differences are related to specific properties of some occupations that have little to do with status and more to do with particular characteristics of the job experience.

In fact, it is difficult to find support in our data for notions that a generic status variable plays any part in the motivational foundations of the decision to vote. The generic formulation of social status underlay the once fashionable idea of "cross-pressures." This idea still appears in print occasionally, as in this recent statement:

> Some persons have an indeterminate status; perhaps their education is high but their income is low, or vice versa. . . . Some scholars speak of such persons as having "cross-pressures" in their status and report that they are less likely to vote than persons who are not cross-pressured. . . . Presumably, for persons in the United States the cross-pressure arises from the tendency for one aspect of their status to incline them in a Republican direction, while the other aspect of their status inclines them toward the Democrats. Some of them resolve the dilemma by not voting at all. [Milbrath and Goel 1977, p. 94]

We found absolutely no evidence for any variant of the cross-pressure hypothesis. While the effect of increments of any single status variable was not always additive, no "inconsistent" combinations were ever related to lower turnout.

The implication of these findings is that an explanation for the relationship between "socioeconomic status" and turnout must have at its core a theory about education's role as a facilitator of voter participation. Education, we have argued, does three things. First, it increases cognitive skills, which facilitates learning about politics. Schooling increases one's capacity for understanding and working with complex, abstract, and intangible subjects such as politics. This heightens one's ability to pay attention to politics, to understand politics, and to gather the information necessary for making political choices. Thus education is a resource that reduces the costs of voting by giving people the skills necessary for processing political information and for making political decisions.

Second, better educated people are likely to get more gratification from political participation. They are more likely to have a strong sense of citizen duty, to feel moral pressure to participate, and to receive expressive benefits from voting.

Finally, schooling imparts experience with a variety of bureaucratic relationships: learning requirements, filling out forms, waiting in lines, and meeting deadlines. This experience helps one overcome the procedural hurdles required first to register and then to vote. In chapter 4 we shall examine further the effect of voter registration provisions on turnout and the reasons why people with more years of formal schooling can more easily overcome the hurdles.

3: AGE AND SEX

The conventional view is that turnout is lowest at the beginning of adult life, rises to a plateau in middle age, and declines as maturity fades into old age (Lipset 1960, p. 189; Flanigan and Zingale 1975, pp. 25–27; Milbrath and Goel 1977, p. 114). In 1972 this pattern held, as figure 3.1 shows.[1] The favorite explanation for declining turnout among the elderly is summarized by Milbrath and Goel: "In the twilight years, physical infirmities probably account for a modest decline in participation" (1977, p. 116). Detailed analysis leads us to question the importance of physical limitations as an explanation of the voting behavior of old people and to revise prevailing notions about the age when the decline sets in, the kinds of old and young people who are most likely to vote, and the reasons for lower turnout among both the old and the young. In order to understand the true relationship between age and voting, we must analyze also the interrelationships of age, sex, and marital status.

Women live longer than men—their life expectancy was nearly eight years higher in 1972—and therefore comprise a larger share of the elderly population. Women are 54 percent of the voting-age population under the age of seventy, 58 percent of those aged seventy to seventy-eight, and 63 percent of people over seventy-eight. Thus we should examine the turnout of men separately from that of women. Figure 3.2, which contrasts the turnout of men and women by age, reveals several important points. First, it shows that in the aggregate, women in 1972 were only 2 percent less likely to vote than men. This contrasts with statements that female turnout is 10 percent (Milbrath and Goel 1977, p. 117) or 6 percent lower (Amundsen 1977, p. 124). Sec-

Figure 3.1. Turnout by Age in 1972

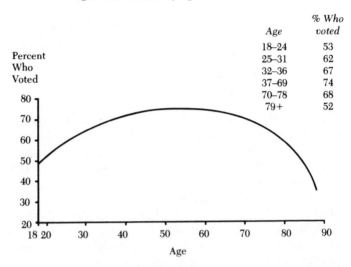

Age	% Who voted
18–24	53
25–31	62
32–36	67
37–69	74
70–78	68
79+	52

ond, women vote as much as men until around the age of forty, when female voting begins to lag slightly. Third, the decline in turnout among the elderly is much steeper for women than for men. Far from losing their capacity to make it to the polling place, men in their seventies continue to vote at about the same rate as middle-aged men. The "twilight years" decline for men does not begin until they are on the threshold of their eightieth year. The turning point for women occurs much earlier in life. Turnout among women in their fifties and sixties is about 5 percent lower than among men, and for women the seventies are a time of decline, a decade in which their voting rate drops substantially below that of men. Only 62 percent of women aged seventy to seventy-eight vote, as compared with 76 percent for their male counterparts. For people over seventy-eight, the turnout rates are 62 percent for men and 46 percent for women—a difference of 16 percentage points.

Figure 3.2. Turnout by Age and Sex in 1972

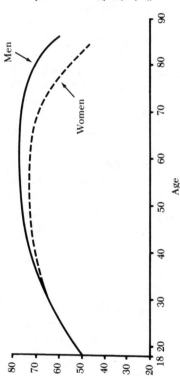

Age	Percent who voted	
	Men	Women
18–24	53	53
	(10,815)	(12,164)
25–31	62	63
	(9,112)	(9,666)
32–36	65	67
	(5,050)	(5,553)
37–69	75	73
	(30,175)	(33,709)
70–78	76	62
	(3,492)	(4,912)
79 and over	62	46
	(1,474)	(2,460)
Total	68	66
	(60,118)	(68,464)

Note: The first number in each cell is the voting rate of the subgroup. The number in parentheses is the weighted number of cases in the subgroup.

One explanation for this disparity is that women more than seventy years old first formed their impressions of appropriate female political roles before the ratification of the Nineteenth Amendment and so might still retain the notion that "voting is for men" (Lane 1959, p. 125). A milder form of this socialization might cause older women to rely more on their husbands for political cues. But because women outlive men, older women will be more likely than men to be living without a spouse. Only 30 percent of women aged seventy or over were married and living with their spouses in 1972, as compared with 73 percent of the men in this age group.[2] To the extent that they rely on their husbands for political cues, older widows might lack the stimulus to vote. So before we can isolate the effect of aging on turnout, we must control for the effect of marital status.

At the same time we might ask whether the presence of a spouse affects turnout at other stages of the life cycle, and for men as well as for women. When we examine the effect of marital status on turnout, it is necessary to keep in mind that the presence of a spouse is related to sex among the elderly and is inversely related to education among the young: uneducated people marry sooner. We must also take into consideration the scantier formal education of older generations. In 1972, 21 percent of people aged eighteen to thirty-six had not graduated from high school, as compared with 42 percent of those between the ages of thirty-seven and sixty-nine and fully 71 percent of those over sixty-nine years old.

Finally, it should be remembered that while income rises through middle age, it declines sharply in old age. In 1972, 80 percent of people at least seventy years old had family incomes under $7,500, almost double the proportion of any other age group with such modest earnings. On the basis of our findings in chapter 2, we do not think that *any* substantial loss of income would necessarily produce an appreciable decline in turnout. But our data also suggest that people whose standards of living are below a minimal level may well be less likely to vote. Thus to isolate the effect of aging from the effect of differences in earning power, we must control for income.

Other researchers have shown that much of the bivariate relationship between age and turnout reflects the presence of some of the other variables we have just discussed. But to the best of our knowledge, no one has held constant all the interrelated variables. The authors of *The American Voter* controlled for education and sex and found "a steady and at times spectacular increase of vote participation as a function of age" (Campbell et al. 1960, p. 494). Their oldest group, however, consisted of everyone over the age of fifty-four. A dozen years later, Verba and Nie (1972, p. 144) found that controlling for education greatly reduced the apparent voting decline of people over sixty-five, while controlling for income actually reversed the trend. Glenn and Grimes (1968, p. 565) report similar findings. On the other hand, a recent study using aggregated cohort data from six Michigan National Election Study samples taken between 1952 and 1972 found that, even with education and sex controls, turnout begins to decline by age sixty and drops off sharply for those over seventy-seven years old (Hout and Knoke 1975).

To summarize: age is related to other demographic characteristics that are related to turnout in at least some circumstances: sex, marital status, education, and income. Using probit analysis, we can control for the effect of these (and other) variables and thus estimate the true relationship between aging and voting participation. We will then be in a better position to judge the merits of several alternative propositions about the reasons why old people do (or do not) vote. This will in turn advance our understanding of broader questions about motivations for voting. We begin with the partial effect of sex on turnout and then examine the effect of marital status. After we understand the relationship of these variables to turnout, we can return to our original question about voting throughout the life cycle.

Sex Differences in Turnout

As we have seen, statements that women are anywhere from 6 to 10 percent less likely to vote than men exaggerate considerably the actual aggregate gap of 2 percent in 1972. With education, income, marital status, and other variables in equation 1 held constant, we can examine more accurately the effect of sex on turnout. In figure 3.3 we graph the partial relationship between age and turnout for men and for women, with other variables held constant. (That is, figure 3.3 is figure 3.2 redrawn after the effect of the other variables in equation 1 was partialed out.) The gap between the curves for men and women represents the partial effect of sex on voting.

Figure 3.3 shows that to the age of forty, men and women vote at virtually the same rate. At about age forty, the turnout of men and women begins to diverge. By age sixty, the turnout gap between the sexes is about 2 percent. The gap widens to 3.5 percent for those between seventy and seventy-eight, and to 4.5 percent for people over age seventy-eight. This difference is small compared to the one we observed in the simple bivariate graph (figure 3.2) for each sex when other variables were not controlled. *Nearly all the differences in turnout between older*

Figure 3.3. Partial Effect of Age on Turnout by Sex

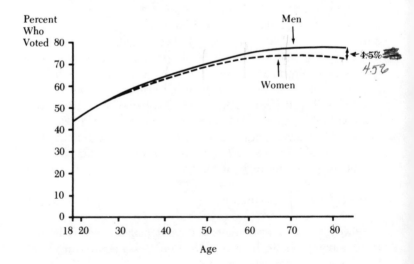

men and women is accounted for by differences in other demographic variables.

The remaining difference in turnout can probably be attributed to the generational differences in the political socialization of women mentioned above. Additional support for this explanation can be found by contrasting our findings with those from the 1952 and 1956 elections reported in *The American Voter* (Campbell et al. 1960, pp. 484–96) and in Converse and Niemi (1971). Controlling for region and education, women aged fifty-five and over were about 14 percent less likely to vote in these elections than their male counterparts.[3] This gap is significantly larger than the one we found for 1972. This change from the 1950s is not an artifact of the more precise and complex data analysis permitted by our larger sample, since even the simple bivariate difference reported in *The American Voter* is not found in our data. Because education was held constant in both analyses, the closing gap is not an artifact of narrowing sex differences in education in the past generation. We think that the shrinking difference between the sexes in turnout stems from the dwindling number of women socialized to political roles that assign predominant influence to men. It seems reasonable to expect, then, that this difference in turnout will soon come close to vanishing as the present oldest cohort of women passes from the scene. Although the attitude that voting is men's business may persist among some old women, it does not seem common among those under sixty. Contrary to the assertion of some feminists, the "ideology of sexism" (Amundsen 1977, p. 137) does not substantially affect voting by women socialized since the adoption of the Nineteenth Amendment.

An alternative explanation has been advanced for why women under sixty now vote at about the same rate as men. Kristi Andersen (1975) argues that this change can be explained by the larger number of working women, because the turnout of women who stay at home lags behind the rates both of employed women and of men. We found no such difference; women who worked were no more likely to vote.[4] Because the difference between male and female turnout is small and concentrated among older people, there is no reason to pursue various other propositions about sex differences in turnout, such as the belief that the gap is widest among the poor, people who live in the country, and Southerners (Converse and Niemi 1971, pp. 445–46).

Marital Status

Married people are more likely to vote than those who are single, separated, divorced, or widowed. The effect of marriage is about the same for men and women, but as table 3.1 shows, it varies considerably with both age and education. For the youngest adults, through the age of twenty-four, marriage raises the likelihood of voting by only about 3 percentage points. The gain in turnout is 5 percent for those aged twenty-five to thirty-one and 6 percent for people who are between the ages of thirty-two and thirty-six. In these younger age groups, the effect of marriage is about the same for all educational levels; college graduates and high school dropouts are equally affected by the presence of a spouse. By the same token, marriage affects educated people similarly at all ages. The relatively small difference observed for the young is also found in middle-aged and elderly college graduates. But for people over thirty-six who have not graduated from college, the effect of marriage increases with age and is greatest among those with less schooling. For people over seventy-eight with only a grammar-school education, not living with a spouse decreases the probability of voting by about 20 percentage points. Among people of the same age with one to three years of college, being without a spouse decreases the probability of voting by 14 percent. In short, marriage leads to higher turnout, and this effect is greatest among old and uneducated people.

One reason for this pattern is suggested in *The American Voter*:

An analysis of interviews with people of very low motivation who have gone to the polls indicates that the most important

Table 3.1. The Effect of Marriage on Turnout, by Age
and Education (in Percent)

Years of education	Age					
	18–24	25–31	32–36	37–69	70–78	78+
0–8 (grammar school)	2	4	5	13	16	20
9–12 (high school)	3	5	7	11	13	17
1–3 college	3	5	8	8	9	14
4 college	3	5	6	6	6	6
5+ college	3	4	4	4	4	a
Total	3	5	6	11	13	19

Note: The entry in each cell is the probit estimate (see appendix C) of the effect on turnout of being married and living with one's spouse, as compared with the voting rate in the given category of people who were single, divorced, widowed, or separated.

[a] Too few cases for analysis.

force on their behavior is interpersonal influence. . . . Personal influence seems particularly important within the family group. [Campbell et al. 1960, p. 109]

Marriage is by far the most important source of this type of influence. People with very little autonomous political motivation are most likely to respond to political stimuli from those with whom they have continuing relationships. Moreover, marriage provides a setting for the reinforcement of one's own beliefs. Spouses are likely to have similar preferences, no matter how feeble. The encouragement of a wife or husband might be the push necessary to get both partners to the polls. If someone has a weak inclination to vote, the presence of another family member who has some tendency in the same direction will raise the probability that both will vote. Glaser (1959) found that it is relatively uncommon for one spouse to vote when the other does not; either both vote or both abstain. He concluded that for many couples the decision to vote is a joint action. This sort of influence is most important where political interest is low. Since interest increases with education, Glaser's finding would explain the greater impact of marriage on the less educated.

The relatively small effect of marriage on young people's voting rates *might* be due *in part* to measurement error. What we have said about the dynamics of personal influence within the family would apply to unmarried couples as well. The Census Bureau estimated that in 1976 about 1.3 million people were living with someone of the opposite sex (*San Francisco Chronicle*, July 27, 1977). We assume that these people are predominantly young and that although they are counted as single, they share the benefits of marriage with respect to voting as well as other aspects of life. The same might be true of another unmarried group of substantial but unknown size—homosexuals living with a member of the same sex. Once again, we assume that these couples are scarcer among the elderly.

Old Age

To this point, our discussion has concentrated on sex differences in turnout, particularly among the elderly. We attributed much of the aggregate decline in voting to generational differences in women's socialization and to the effect of living without a spouse, and we saw that changes in both marital status and the effect of marital status are a function of age. We have also noted that the elderly have less education and lower incomes. We can now look at our original question: what is the effect of growing older, in and of itself, on the likelihood of voting?

Before discussing the probit coefficients on which we base our estimates of the effect of age (and youth) on turnout, it is useful to look at table 3.2, which depicts the cross-tabulation between turnout and age, controlling only for education. Table 3.2 shows a gain in turnout for people aged seventy to seventy-eight in several educational categories, and in only one group—people with four years of college—is there a drop of more than 2 percentage points. Thus the education control alone reduces most of the "twilight years" decline suggested by the bivariate relationship depicted in figure 3.1.

The multivariate analysis made possible by probit analysis is

Table 3.2.   Turnout by Age and Education, in 1972 (in Percent)

Years of education	Age						
	18–24	25–31	32–36	37–69	70–78	78+	Total
0–8 (grammar school)	14	26	36	56	58	44	52
9–12 (high school)	44	55	63	75	76	63	65
1–3 college	72	76	79	87	85	72	79
4 college	76	84	89	90	85	75	86
5+ college	85	86	91	93	94	80	91
Total	53	62	67	74	68	52	67

Note: These are simple cross-tabulations using the entire sample. The entry in each cell is the percentage of people voting with the given combination of age and education. For example, 36 percent of people aged thirty-two to thirty-six who had not attended high school voted.

summarized in figure 3.4. It shows that once other demographic variables have been held constant, *aging, by itself, produces not a decline but an increase in turnout.* The rate of increase in voting begins to level off at around age fifty-five but turnout continues to rise, at an increasingly slower pace, through the seventies.[5] The decline in turnout among people over sixty shown in figure 3.1 is explained not by their greater age but by differences in education, marital status, and sex.[6] This permits us to reject explanations that "interpret the decline in vote turnout among the very old to reflect the onset of physical infirmities and a narrowing of psychological participation in the broader life of the society as senility approaches" (Converse and Niemi 1971, p. 445).

Our finding that turnout increases with age is not unique. Some other researchers have reported the same thing (Campbell et al. 1960, pp. 493–97; Glenn and Grimes 1968) but offer very different explanations for their finding. Glenn and Grimes turn upside down the familiar "disengagement hypothesis," that old age brings a progressive withdrawal from society and hence a reduced likelihood of voting. They accept the fact of disengagement but argue that far from portending a decline in voting, it

Figure 3.4. Partial Effect of Age on Turnout

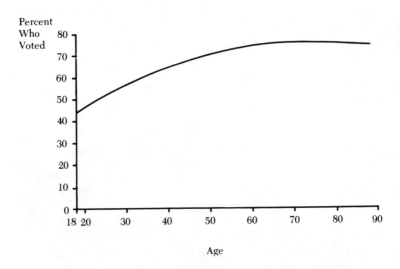

Percent
Who
Voted

brings higher turnout rates because political participation fills
the void left by the cessation of other commitments. Their
argument touches on a major theoretical approach to turnout and
hence is worth quoting at length:

> . . . an increase in political interest may compensate for
> loss of opportunity or inclination to attend to other interests.
> . . . A related hypothesis is that political interest is inversely
> related to degree of involvment with personal problems and
> ambitions, the exigencies of day-to-day living, and non-
> political interests. . . . When the husband retires, both male
> and female have all too little with which to be preoccupied.
> . . . For many, attention to politics becomes a functional
> substitute for the activites and concerns that absorbed so
> much time and energy earlier. . . . we believe the primary
> explanation [for variations in turnout among individuals of
> different age] is the difference at various stages of the life cy-
> cle in distracting influences and the need to compensate for

lack of other activities and interests. Variation in distracting influences can also help explain differences in political participation by sex and social level. Certainly, the exigencies of day-to-day living are typically more urgent at the lower social levels, and the day-to-day tasks of the typical housewife and mother are less clearly related to most political issues, and thus perhaps more distracting from politics, than the occupational tasks of her husband. [Glenn and Grimes 1968, pp. 564, 573, 574]

Implicit in this explanation are several assumptions about the turnout of various demographic categories that are contradicted by our data: housewives do not vote less than working women or than men; the turnout of people in the "lower social levels" is explained primarily by their educational attainments. More important, our findings provide no evidence for the proposition that people with less free time or more "other activities and interests" are less likely to vote. Indeed, the opposite is the case. Whenever we know the relative amount of free time available to different demographic categories, it is invariably the case that turnout is higher in groups with *less* free time. The same is true of other pursuits. The types of people who vote most heavily are also most likely to belong to and participate in organizations (Barnes 1977).

The authors of *The American Voter* take a different tack to explain why turnout increases with age:

. . . the motivational differences that arise as a result of education are not the same as the processes that draw disproportionate numbers of older people to the polls. . . .
None of the major motivational terms [political involvement or a sense of political efficacy or citizen duty] intervening between increased education and higher vote turnout vary systematically by age in a manner that would convince us that they are intervening terms here as well. [Campbell et al. 1960, pp. 494–95]

We have no quarrel with the notion that involvement in an elec-

toral outcome heightens turnout (see chapter 2). But the statement about different motivational foundations is not supported
by more detailed analysis of the data. Analyzing the Michigan
1972 election data, we also found no consequential relationships
between age and such "motivational terms" as interest in the
campaign and in politics, use of the mass media, and political information. This finding is hardly conclusive, however, because
of the marked inverse relationship between age and education.
When we controlled for education, we found that among people
who had not attended college, age brought a substantial increase
in political interest, use of the mass media, and political information. There were no such relationships among the college educated. In fact, political knowledge declined with age among this
group. We will return to these findings when we discuss increases in turnout in the early and middle part of the life cycle.
Here it is sufficient to note that age and education do indeed
seem related to a similar motivational pattern.

The Effect of Mobility on Turnout

A glance at figure 3.4 should remove any doubts about
the conventional wisdom that the young are light voters. The
multivariate analysis that disconfirmed the notion of declining
turnout by the elderly strengthens the relationship between
youth and nonvoting. Controlling for other demographic characteristics, people aged eighteen to twenty-four are about 28 percent less likely to vote than fifty-five-year-olds; those aged
twenty-five to thirty-one are about 21 percentage points less
likely to vote.

We observed in chapter 2 that the relationships of education,
income, and occupation to turnout were very similar in 1972 and
1974, with the exception of a smaller decline by farmers from
presidential to midterm years. A more substantial exception is in
the turnout of young people. The relationship of age to turnout is
even stronger in midterm than in presidential elections. The disparity can most easily be seen in the age composition of the

voting populations in the two years. People under the age of
thirty-two comprised 28 percent of the voters in 1972 and just 22
percent of those voting in the 1974 election.

Attempts to explain low turnout by the young generally rely on
phrases like "settling down." This expression alludes not only to
the "restlessness" of the young but to their greater mobility and
the "specific legal obstacles to voting associated with short residence" (Verba and Nie 1972, p. 139). The young do indeed move
more often than the rest of the population, and we will postpone
a direct look at their voting patterns until we consider the question of mobility. To do so we must shift to the 1974 census survey, since the 1972 study did not ascertain mobility. As table 3.3
shows, the relationship between youth and residential mobility is
very strong. Nearly 60 percent of people under the age of thirty-
two had moved within the previous two years, that is, between
the 1972 and 1974 elections. This compares with 39 percent of
those thirty-two to thirty-six, 19 percent of people aged thirty-
seven to sixty-nine, and just 14 percent of those older than sixty-
nine. Approximately 20 percent of college graduates moved
between elections, as compared with 11 percent of those who
had not attended college.

Before 1972, movers often ran afoul of statutes that required a
year or more of residency before one was eligible to vote. But by

Table 3.3. Age and Length of Residence in 1974 (in Percent)

Length of residence at current address	Age					
	18–24	25–31	32–36	37–69	70–78	78+
Under 4 months	18%	12%	7%	3%	3%	2%
4–11 months	19	18	11	5	4	4
1–2 years	20	30	21	11	8	8
3–5 years	11	25	26	15	10	11
6–9 years	8	9	21	16	13	11
10+ years	25	6	15	50	62	64
Total	101%	100%	101%	100%	100%	100%

Note: The entry in each cell is the percentage of people in the indicated age category who had lived at their current address for the indicated length of time.

the 1972 election, legislation and court decisions had abolished these requirements, and all but two states had residency requirements of no more than a month. As we will see in chapter 4, the remaining residency requirements had no effect on turnout in 1972. The important legal restriction is the closing date—the deadline for registration. This, too, is effectively limited in much the same way as residency requirements.

Although these reforms removed the legal impediments to voting for people who had moved at least a month prior to the election, changing residences still has a pronounced negative effect on the probability of voting, as table 3.4 shows. When we hold all other demographic variables constant, people who had lived at their current address for less than four months before the 1974 election were 23 percentage points less likely to vote than those who had not moved for at least ten years. For those who had spent one to two years in the new home, the rate was still 19 percent lower. After two years, however, the effect of mobility declines sharply. People who had moved three to five years prior to the 1974 election were only 9 percent less likely to vote than those who had remained in the same place for ten years or more.

It is easy to understand why the effect on turnout is greatest among those who have moved fairly recently. As Lane points out,

Table 3.4. Effect on Turnout of Mobility, by Age, in 1974 (in Percent)

	Length of residence at current address				
Age	Less than 4 months	4–11 months	1–2 years	3–5 years	6–9 years
18–24	−17	−15	−12	−4	−2
25–31	−23	−23	−19	−8	0
32–36	−28	−26	−21	−9	−1
37–69	−31	−28	−23	−11	−2
70+	−26	−23	−18	−8	0
Total	−23	−22	−19	−9	−1

Note: The entry in each cell is the probit estimate (see appendix C) of the effect on turnout of living at one's current residence for the indicated length of time, compared to the turnout of those in the same age group who have not moved in ten or more years.

"people who first come into a community are likely to have fewer associational ties, less information on community affairs, few political contacts, fewer emotional and material stakes in the group tensions that express themselves in politics" (1959, p. 267). Relocation also requires a period of adjustment: furnishing and remodeling a new home, adopting new school and business schedules, meeting neighbors and locating merchants and services. When so many other concerns demand immediate attention, there is little time to think about politics.

In addition to preoccupation with adjustment to a new environment, even the simplest initial political activity—such as registering to vote—may be difficult, even if one can do so at a convenient hour or in one's own neighborhood. The low turnout of people who moved more than four months before the election cannot be explained by legal disenfranchisement; no state had residence requirements or closing dates that prevented registering more than sixty days before election day, and most had a cutoff date fewer than thirty days before. In addition, people who had moved one to two years before the election voted only a bit more than those who had moved four months earlier. Therefore the need to reestablish eligibility, in and of itself, is the hurdle to be overcome.

The fact that the effect of moving drops sharply to 9 percent for those who have lived at their new address for three to five years suggests that the excitement of a presidential election may be necessary to bring many people back to the registration rolls. The weaker stimulus of a midterm election does not seem to motivate many people who have moved since the last election to register and vote. If subsequent research finds that residential mobility does not have such a big effect on turnout in presidential elections, then we will have identified an intervening variable —residential mobility and the need to re-register—that helps explain lower midterm election turnout and the disproportionately small number of young voters in such elections. Midterm voting may be lighter partly because the third of the population that has moved since the last presidential election is about 20 percent less likely to vote than those who have not moved in the same period.

If this speculation is correct, any sort of legal change that removed the need to re-register after a move would have its most drastic impact on turnout in midterm rather than presidential elections.

As table 3.4 shows, moving does not have the same effect on everybody. Although the young are the most likely to move, they are the least affected by it. Compared to those who have stayed put for at least ten years, people aged eighteen to twenty-four who move between elections are 17 percent less likely to vote, while the effect of moving on people between the ages of thirty-seven and sixty-nine is a drop of 31 percentage points in the probability of voting. This suggests that it is the relative cost of relocation that affects turnout. In early adulthood, moving is less burdensome; there are fewer family and social obligations, fewer possessions, and fewer financial interests. But as people age, their wider range of possessions, interests, and associations —equity in a home, business contacts, friends and leisure activities, organization memberships, and children in school—make it more difficult for them to move. Thus the costs of moving for people in this age group are greater than for either the young or the old.

A similar pattern emerges when we examine the effect of moving on people with different amounts of education. The impact of a recent change of residence is greatest on the most educated. A move within a year of the election trims the turnout of those with college degrees by 8 percent more than it reduces the turnout of those who have not attended college. The difference in impact disappears by the second year after moving. Like the middle-aged, the better educated face greater costs when they move.

In summary, mobility substantially decreases the probability that an individual will vote. A midterm election is not interesting enough to motivate many recent movers to register and vote. The costs of acquiring voting information in a new, unfamiliar community are high, and the low stimulus of an off-year election provides little incentive to do so.

Youth and "Adult Roles"

Frequent changes of residence explain only part of the turnout gap between young people and their elders. (See also Verba and Nie 1972, p. 146.) There are substantial disparities in the voting rates of people of different age who lived in the same place for equal amounts of time. At any given length of residence, people aged thirty-seven to sixty-nine are one and one-half to two times more likely to vote than the youngest adults.

Geographical mobility is only one aspect of settling down, however. The following passage suggests other elements in a familiar line of argument:

> Political interest demands "eyes turned outward"—a capacity to devote some attention to events outside one's immediate daily life yet which are significant for the broader community. Young single persons in their twenties are inevitably preoccupied with two rather personal quests: the quest for a mate and the quest for a suitable job. These quests are to some degree incompatible with devotion of attention to broader events. Once a mate is found—and this usually means some kind of tolerable job as well—the individual begins to take a more stable role in adult life and can afford to turn his eyes outward in a new degree. It is at this point that his interest in what is going on in politics first begins to mature. [Converse and Niemi 1971, p. 461]

In a similar vein, Milbrath and Goel say, "The most apathetic group are the young unmarried citizens who are only marginally integrated into their community" (1977, p. 115). They conclude:

> The full array of data suggests, then, that there are three intervening variables relating age to participation: integration with the community, the availability of blocks of free time for politics, and good health. Integration with the community develops gradually with marriage, job responsibility, and acquiring a family; thus, participation rises gradually

with advancing age, leveling off at about thirty-five or forty.
[Milbrath and Goel 1977, p. 116]

In short, the hypothesis is that voting goes up when young
people take on adult roles. Married young people are presumably more settled and "adult" than their single counterparts. The
adult-role hypothesis would lead us to expect substantial increases in turnout amoung young married couples. But as table
3.1 shows, the effect of marriage on turnout is weakest on young
people and increases steadily with age. Turnout among married
couples eighteen to twenty-four years old is only 3 percent more
than among their unmarried peers; it is 5 percent greater
for those aged twenty-five to thirty-one. This may be compared
with a difference of 11 percent in the group of people thirty-
seven to sixty-nine years old and substantially higher amounts for
the elderly. Even if we think that this gap for young couples is
depressed by significant numbers of unmarried relationships, it
is difficult to find much support in these figures for the notion
that adult roles have much to do with voting. To the extent that
living together is a pastime of the young—something that one
grows out of—getting married may be taken as an index of assuming an adult role, and thus we are back to the fact that marriage
has less effect on turnout among the young than among anyone
else. From this, we interpret the relationship between marriage
and turnout as a matter of mutual reinforcement, not of adult-
role assumption. However "adult" is defined, we assume that attaining this status is not a process that consumes much of the individual's life.

Another way to test the adult-role hypothesis is to compare
students with those who are no longer in school. If the hypothesis holds, one would expect less voting among students than
among people who have been in the adult world of the job market. In estimating the effect on turnout of being a student, we
again used equation 1 to hold constant all other variables. Among
people eighteen to twenty-four years old, students vote at a
much *higher* rate than nonstudents. Students with fewer than
four years of college vote 20 percentage points more than others

with the same amount of education. College graduates who are still in school vote 16 percent more than those with the same amount of education who are no longer in the university. Students who have completed at least a year of graduate school are 14 percent more likely to vote than their nonstudent counterparts. To the extent that leaving school measures the assumption of an adult role, these findings are totally inconsistent with the proposition that young people will vote more as they assume adult roles and set aside childish things like school.

Why do students vote so much more than nonstudents? Being part of a college community provides relatively free access to information about politics. Through living groups, extracurricular activities, and classes, students are less socially isolated than nonstudents. Furthermore, not only is political information freer, but it is generally easier for students to register and vote. Often both can be done on campus or in immediately adjacent residential and commercial neighborhoods. It might be argued that 1972 was a particularly active year for electioneering on campus because of McGovern's appeal to students. Still, our analysis of turnout in 1974, when McGovern had passed from the political scene, indicates that students still voted more than nonstudents, although the difference was only about a quarter of that found for 1972. The turnout gap between students and nonstudents was not just a passing phenomenon in 1972.

In short, community norms, social interaction, and the lower costs of registering and voting all facilitate student turnout. When people leave the university, they generally enter a less politically stimulating environment. While this move certainly does not reduce the individual's relevant skills, it is likely to increase the costs of registering and voting and will perhaps also provide less normative support for doing so.

These data suggest a modification of the familiar assumption about turnout during the life cycle. First, among the college educated, instead of a steady rise in turnout, beginning with entry into the electorate, there is a dip after leaving school, followed by a gain continuing to the mid-fifties plateau. Second, we find no

support for the position that turnout among young people increases as they assume adult roles. Being married has the
smallest effect on the young. Those who have just entered the
adult world of jobs and careers voted less, not more, than those
still in school. Third, one should not include "lack of time"
among the conditions of early adult life that militate against
voting. For the reasons mentioned earlier, we doubt that many
people fail to vote because they cannot spare the time. Moreover, time-use studies find that young people have more leisure
time than older citizens do (Stafford and Duncan 1977, table 8).

One final observation should be made about low turnout
among the young. It has been argued that the eighteen-year-old
vote was the reason for the aggregate decline in turnout of 5.2
percentage points between 1968 and 1972. Turnout in 1972 was
52 percent for the eighteen- to twenty-year-olds and 54 percent
for the twenty-one to twenty-four-year-olds, who would have
been eligible to vote regardless of the Twenty-sixth Amendment.
By removing the eighteen- to twenty-year-olds from our full
sample, we can recompute what turnout would have been in
1972 if the eighteen-year-old vote had not been instituted.[7]
Doing so raises the national level of turnout by only 1.2 percentage points. In other words, the eighteen-year-old vote accounted
at most for one-quarter of the drop in turnout between 1968 and
1972.

Turnout and the Life Cycle

To explain the rise in turnout with increasing age that we observe in figure 3.4, we must look at people by their level of educational attainment. In figure 3.5 we have redrawn figure 3.4
separately for each education group. As we see in figure 3.5, the
life-cycle patterns of turnout are very different for people of
varying educational attainments. Voting by people who have not
been to college increases about 30 percentage points between
the earliest years of eligibility and age fifty-five, with all other
variables controlled. The corresponding increase for college drop-

outs is 23 percent; for college graduates, 16 percent; and only 11 percent for those with postgraduate training. In other words, the effect of age on the probability of voting is greatest among those with the least schooling. The effect of age shrinks as years of formal schooling increase. (The steeper the curve in figure 3.5, the greater the effect of age on turnout.) In addition, by looking at the differences in turnout between educational groups at different age levels, one can observe that education has the greatest effect on turnout among the young and its effect diminishes progressively with age.

We have argued that people who have skill and experience in dealing with complex and intangible subjects are more likely to vote. Education is one source of ability to understand politics. In addition, schooling increases one's interest in politics and imparts experience with bureaucratic relationships. The young who have been to college are more likely to possess these skills and experiences than are their counterparts whose education

Figure 3.5. Partial Effect of Age on Turnout by Education Level

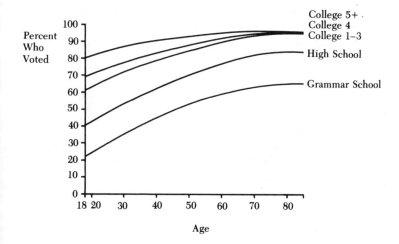

stopped with elementary or high school. Trying to explain why people in some occupations (farmers, clerks, and salespeople) voted more than we would expect, given their education, we suggested that such jobs often provided substitutes for education, experiences that taught skills other people learn in school. Our findings about the greater effect of aging on the uneducated point to another source of these skills—exposure to life in general and politics in particular. As Converse and Niemi wrote, "It is as though accumulated adult experience begins slowly to make up for their abbreviated *formal* educations" (1971, p. 449; emphasis in original). Life experience is a substitute for school. Many uneducated people, who have the fewest politically relevant skills when they become eligible to vote, become more accomplished in coping with bureaucratic hurdles and thinking about political material. Consistent with this assertion is the previously noted increase in political interest, information, and use of the mass media among older people without the benefit of a college education and the lack of any such change in those who have gone to college.

In other words, the start-up costs of voting are not borne equally by all young people. The cost of entering the political system is relatively small for the educated, but for those without such skills the costs are nearly three times as great. Many people in this group learn by the experience of continued exposure to politics as they grow older.

4: THE EFFECT OF
REGISTRATION LAWS
ON TURNOUT

Most Americans, in order to vote, must first establish their eligibility by registering prior to election day.[1] Any time someone moves, he must usually re-register at his new address. Registration raises the costs of voting. Citizens must first perform a separate task that lacks the immediate gratification characterizing other forms of political expression (such as voting). Registration is usually more difficult than voting, often involving more obscure information and a longer journey at a less convenient time, to complete a more complicated procedure. Moreover, it must usually be done before interest in the campaign has reached its peak. Converse and Niemi nicely describe the burden of registration:

> . . . it is hard to forget that it is Election Day. . . . The process of prior registration, on the other hand, is much more diffuse and vaguely defined. Most people know that there is some kind of deadline, perhaps, but few people would know just when it was or where it was necessary to go. [1971, p. 456]

Each state determines its own registration laws, subject only to certain limitations imposed by the U.S. Constitution, court decisions, and national legislation. Despite these limitations (many of which are quite recent), the states differ widely in the extent to which registration increases the costs of voting. Residency requirements vary from one day to two months. In some states one can register until the weekend before election day; in others, the closing date falls when the election is still a month away. Some states register voters only at a county office that is open a few

61

hours a week, when most people are working; other states require offices to remain open at night or on Saturdays, authorize
registration at many convenient locations, or do both.

These state-by-state variations are an opportunity to test our
theory of who votes, which emphasizes the costs of performing
the minor bureaucratic tasks required to cast a ballot and asserts
that ability to surmount these hurdles is aided by skills learned in
school. Our theory suggests two propositions about the electoral
impact of registration laws:

1. Turnout will be lower where the obstacles to voting are
greater.
2. Variations in the difficulty of registering will make the most
difference to people least able to cope with bureaucratic
problems—those with the least education.

There are two explanations for the second proposition. First, education increases political interest. Schooling provides information about public issues and greater capacity to understand them.
Therefore better educated people are more likely to be interested enough to overcome the inconveniences of limited office
hours and earlier deadlines. Second, the bureaucratic skills ac-
quired in school reduce the difficulty of overcoming these hurdles. In other words, the likelihood that an individual will vote is
not merely a behavioral manifestation of certain individual im-
pulses. It also reflects the ease with which these individual pre-
dilections can be expressed in action. More education produces
both a bigger incentive to jump the hurdle and a lower hurdle.

In addition to its scholarly value, information on these points is
useful in the continuing public debate about the desirability of
revising election laws in order to increase voting rates.[2] The first
step in our analysis will be a description of the several areas of legal regulation of voter registration.

State Suffrage Laws, 1960–1973

1. *Poll taxes*. In 1960 some Southern states imposed a tax as a
condition for registration. A few states made the tax liability cu-

mulative, that is, before being allowed to register, an individual had to pay the tax not only for the current year but for all earlier years of his eligibility for which fees remained unpaid. The Twenty-fourth Amendment to the Constitution prohibited poll taxes in federal elections in 1964. Two years later the Supreme Court abolished the practice altogether (*Harper* v. *Virginia State Board of Elections*, 1966).

2. *Literacy tests.* Most common in the South, these varied in nature, depending on state requirements ranging from simple literacy to a demand that the applicant interpret a provision of the state or federal constitution. Inequitable administration of the tests was the principal means of disenfranchising Southern blacks. Literacy tests were suspended in much of the South by the Voting Rights Act of 1965. They were abolished everywhere by the Voting Rights Act Amendments (VRAA) of 1970.

3. *Permanent or periodic registration.* In 1960 a number of states required potential voters to re-register at intervals of as little as one year. By 1972 only two states required re-registration, and the prescribed interval in both was ten years. A few states allowed re-registration at the discretion of local officials. This option has been exercised in a couple of Southern states, presumably as a means of reducing black turnout (Reitman and Davidson 1972, pp. 33–34).

4. *Purging for nonvoting.* Similar to rules calling for periodic registration is the requirement that people who have not voted within a stated time be dropped from the registration rolls. The period ranges from two to eight years. Some states have no purging provision at all.

5. *Residency requirements.* In the early 1960s thirty-eight states required at least a year's residence in the state before one could register. The 1970 Voting Rights Act Amendments in effect imposed a maximum thirty-day residency requirement for presidential elections. They also permitted new residents to vote in their previous state either in person or by absentee ballot. In March 1972 the Supreme Court, in *Dunn* v. *Blumstein*, struck down Tennessee's one-year requirement. As a result of this decision, residency requirements for other elections were restricted.

Although the Court did not impose a new limit, its decision was interpreted as strongly suggesting a maximum residency requirement of thirty days before the election.

6. *Closing date*. This is the last day one can register before the election—the date registration is closed. The 1970 VRAA mandated a closing date at most thirty days before presidential elections. The Court's decision in *Dunn* v. *Blumstein* noted that for other elections "30 days appears to be an ample period of time" (*Dunn* v. *Blumstein* 1972). But a year later the Court permitted Arizona and Georgia to retain their longer closing dates (*Marston* v. *Lewis* 1973; and *Burns* v. *Fortson* 1973). It is easy to confuse closing dates and residency requirements, and the two are, of course, interdependent.

7. *Regular office hours*. Most states require registration offices to remain open Monday through Friday during normal business hours. Other states either impose less stringent schedules or are silent on this subject. Thus offices in some states may be open only a few hours on some days of the week, drastically reducing opportunities for registration.

8. *Evening and Saturday registration*. Recognizing that most people work during the day from Monday to Friday, many states require that registration offices be open after normal working hours, on Saturday, or both.

9. *County, city, or neighborhood offices*. In some states potential voters can register only at the county seat. Other states provide registration offices located in each city. Most convenient is neighborhood registration, usually in firehouses, libraries, and the like.

10. *Deputy registrars*. Some states authorize deputizing ordinary citizens to register voters. Deputy registrars go from house to house, set up tables in shopping centers, and so on. Such provisions are often exploited by political parties and interest groups, which supply deputy registrars.

11. *Absentee registration*. The 1970 VRAA required all states to permit absentee registration in presidential elections solely on grounds of absence from one's place of residence. This is a mini-

mum standard. Some states permit absentee registration for various other reasons, and a few authorize it for anyone. Federal postcard registration would authorize nationwide absentee registration. A major question in congressional debate was whether postcards should be mailed to everyone or whether the individual should have to take action to obtain a postcard.[3] The latter alternative resembles the system used by five states in 1972.

The dozen years before the 1972 election saw broad liberalization of registration requirements. Poll taxes and literacy tests were abolished; periodic registration vanished, except for ten-year re-registration in Arizona and South Carolina; residency requirements were measured in days rather than years; closing dates were closer to election day; and there were minimum national standards for absentee registration. Some observers and politicians thought that these changes had eliminated the flaws in the registration procedure (Phillips and Blackman 1975; Tarrance, 1976). Others asserted, "Our current voter registration laws are a scandal and a national disgrace" (Kennedy 1975) and result "in disenfranchisement on a massive scale" (McGee 1975). This debate was part of attempts at both state and federal levels to ease the burden of registration further. The Carter administration's unsuccessful 1977 proposal for election day registration was the latest indication of this movement. Like bills for nationwide postcard registration in 1971, 1973, 1975, and 1976, it foundered in Congress on opposition by Republicans and Southern Democrats.

Estimating the Impact of Registration Laws on Turnout

One reason for the level of controversy about the new legislative proposals was the difficulty of establishing the extent to which existing provisions were an obstacle to voting.[4] It might be thought that people could simply be asked whether they were discouraged by registration requirements, as at least one scholar (Sterling 1979) recommended. The Census Bureau asks its unregistered respondents why they did not register; this information is available. The drawback to such an approach is that one cannot have much confidence in the answers. The Census Bureau had this to say about responses to the question in 1966:[5]

> Failure to meet residence requirements was cited by only 7 percent of those persons with less than 8 years of schooling, but was the most common reason for not registering (42 percent) given by respondents who were college graduates. This may well reflect the fact that people with little education are not aware of the residence laws for voting or do not know what they require, and, therefore, are more accurately categorized as apathetic. College graduates, on the other hand, may be tempted to give residence requirements as a reason, rather than reporting a less acceptable reason. [U.S. Bureau of the Census 1968, p. 3]

Analyzing our data for 1972, we found no relationship between the actual permissiveness of a state's laws and the proportion of state residents who said they were unregistered because they could not satisfy the residency requirement or because they had been unable to register. Converse and Niemi found that some respondents who said they had not voted because they were not registered lived in places where registration was not required (1971, p. 456). Similarly, in 1972 one-third of the nonvoting respondents from North Dakota (a state which did not have voter registration) cited restrictive registration provisions as the reason why they did not participate.

Another method of assessing the impact of registration laws is to compare states with notably high and notably low turnouts. Table 4.1 lists this information for the 1972 election. Using this approach, we might examine the laws in the ten states with the lowest turnout, where just 38 to 48 percent of the voting-age citizens cast a ballot for a presidential candidate. Only two of these states have closing dates less than a month before the election, and only two require that registration offices remain open in the evening or on Saturday. In the ten states with the highest turnout (64 to 69 percent), on the other hand, closing dates tend to be nearer election day, and most require evening and/or Saturday registration. The problem with this approach is that the low turnout states are all in the South. Southerners are less educated on the average than are other Americans, and thus we would expect them to vote less, irrespective of the difficulty of registering. It is also possible, of course, that lower Southern turnout in part reflects attempts by local officials to impede black voting. Finally, there is the problem of sorting out which aspects of registration laws make a difference. Are the critical factors residency requirements, closing dates, the time when one can register, the place where one must go, the availability of absentee registration, or some combination of these and other areas of variation? Numerous combinations are possible, and the actual patterns in the fifty states are far from random. States that have restrictive provisions affecting one aspect of registration are likely to have restrictive provisions bearing on other aspects. Thus, to estimate the effect on turnout of a particular registration requirement, the other legal provisions and the demographic variables must be held constant.

Probit analysis is the best way to estimate the effect of each statute, and the Census Bureau's 1972 sample provides enough respondents in each state to do so. The probit subsample for the effect of registration laws is not the same one that we used for our other data analyses. We designed it to maximize the variation among registration requirements, thus improving the estimates of their impact on turnout.[6] We ignored the weighting factor and, within each state, randomly selected actual respondents. We chose about 150 respondents per state for most states.[7] (Alaska, Nevada, and Vermont each had fewer than 150 respondents, all of whom were picked.) Seven states with unusual combinations of registration provisions were oversampled to increase further the variation in the independent variables. Alabama, Arkansas, Georgia, Idaho, Louisiana, and Utah were oversampled by 50 percent; and all 202 respondents from North Dakota were included. The resulting subsample of 7,936 actual respondents was used in all analyses of census data in this chap-

Table 4.1. State Turnout and Registration Laws in 1972

State	Turnout [a]	Residency requirement (days)	Closing date— days before election	Where to register [b]	Deputy registrars allowed	Registration office open 40 hours a week	Evening and/or Saturday registration required	Absentee registration [c]	Years of nonvoting before purging from rolls
Utah	69.4	31	11	C		X	X	X	4
South Dakota	68.9	15	15	T	X	X	X	X	4
Minnesota	68.9	30	20	T	X	X	X	X	4
Connecticut	68.6	7	24	P	X	X	X	X	None
North Dakota	68.2	10			No Registration [d]			X	2
Montana	68.1	30	30	P	X	X		X	2
New Hampshire	65.5	30	9	T				X	None
Massachusetts	65.2	29	28	T	X	X	X	X	None
Washington	65.1	31	31	P	X	X		e	2.5
Illinois	64.2	30	28	P	X	X	X	U	4
Wyoming	64.1	30	15	T		X		X	2
Idaho	63.8	3	3	P	X	X		U	8
Iowa	63.6	10	10	P	X	X	X	X	4
Rhode Island	63.5	30	30	T	X	X	X	X	5
California	63.0	7	30	P	X	X	X	X	2
Delaware	63.0	17	17	P	X	X	X	X	4
West Virginia	62.7	30	29	C		X		X	2.4
Wisconsin	62.5	1	13/20 [f]	T	X	X		X	2
Oregon	62.5	1	31	P	X	X		X	None

State									
Vermont	62.3	30	3	T	X	X	X		X	None
Maine	62.2	30	8[g]	T	X	X	X		X	None
New Jersey	62.0	30	40	T	X	X			X	4
Indiana	61.2	30	29	P		X			X	2
Colorado	60.8	29	32	P	X	X	X		X	2
Michigan	60.6	30	30	T	X	X	X		X	4
Kansas	59.3	1	20	C	X	X			X	2
New York	59.1	30	24	P	X	X			X	2
New Mexico	58.3	30	42	P	X	X			X	2
Ohio	58.1	14	13	C	X	X			X	2
Missouri	57.8	30	28	T	X	X				4[g]
Oklahoma	57.2	15	11	P	X	X				2/4[h]
Pennsylvania	56.6	30	31	T	X	X			X	2
Nebraska	56.3	2	11	C	X	X			X	4
Hawaii	54.2	26	26	P	X				U	2
Nevada	51.9	30	38	C	X	X				2
Florida	51.3	30	31	T	X	X	X	X		2
Maryland	51.1	30	29	T	X				X	5
Arizona	49.0	30	50	P		X			X	2
Alaska	48.9	30	30	P	X	X			X	4
Kentucky	48.5	30	30	T		X			U	2
Arkansas	47.9	30	20	C	X	X				4
Texas	46.2	61	30	C	X				X	3
Virginia	45.9	30	30	T		X			U	None
Mississippi	45.1	30	30	C	X	X				None
Louisiana	44.6	30	30	C	X		X		X	4
Tennessee	43.7	50	30	C			X	X	X	4

Table 4.1 (continued)

State	Turn-out[a]	Residency requirement (days)	Closing date—days before election	Where to register[b]	Deputy registrars allowed	Registration office open 40 hours a week	Evening and/or Saturday registration required	Absentee registration[c]	Years of nonvoting before purging from rolls
Alabama	43.6	11	11	C				X	None
North Carolina	43.6	4	29	P		X			4
South Carolina	38.7	30	31	C	X	X			4
Georgia	38.1	30	50	C	X	X		X	3

Note: See appendix D for sources and coding procedures.

[a] Percentage of citizens of voting age who cast a ballot in the presidential election. *Source:* U.S. Bureau of the Census, "Language Minority, Illiteracy, and Voting Data Used in Making Determinations for the Voting Rights Act Amendments of 1975 (Public Law 94–73)," *Current Population Reports, Population Characteristics,* U.S. Department of Commerce, series P-25, no. 627; and letter to the authors from Gilbert R. Felton, U.S. Bureau of the Census, Population Division, December 29, 1976.

[b] C = county only; T = town or city; P = precinct or neighborhood.

[c] U = universal absentee registration; X = permitted for absence and/or illness.

[d] Closing date was coded "0." Where to register was coded "P." Deputy registrars was coded "allowed." Registration office open forty hours a week was coded "open forty hours a week." Evening and/or Saturday registration was coded "required." Absentee registration was coded "universal." Years of nonvoting before purging from rolls was coded "none."

[e] Only permitted if absent from county but residing within the state, and then not by mail.

[f] Respondents living in the central cities of SMSAs under 1 million persons were coded "20." All other respondents were coded "13."

[g] Some intrastate variation that cannot be specifically coded.

[h] Respondents living in the central cities and suburbs of SMSAs under 1 million persons were coded "2."

ter. Our coding procedures and the source of our data on individual state registration laws are described in appendix D.

The variables in our initial probit equation, together with the probit estimates and standard errors, are in appendix E. When education and region are controlled, race has no independent effect on turnout and so was dropped from the final probit equation for registration laws—equation 2, in appendix F. Four registration provisions had a consequential impact on the probability of voting in the initial equation and therefore were included in equation 2: (a) closing date; (b) regular hours for registration offices; (c) requiring offices to be open in the evening and/or on Saturdays; and (d) the availability of absentee registration. Two other variables were included in the final equation because they had a small positive correlation with both the statutes and turnout: the hours the polls were open on election day and a concurrent gubernatorial election in the state.[8]

The effect of existing registration laws on the probability of *individuals* voting in 1972 is summarized in appendix G. The provision with the largest impact is the closing date. Depending on the probability that one would otherwise vote, a thirty-day closing date decreased the likelihood of voting by 3 to 9 percentage points. (Remember that in probit analysis the estimated effect of an independent variable depends on the probability that the individual would otherwise vote.) A fifty-day closing date (in effect in Arizona and Georgia) lowered the probability of voting by about 17 percent for people with a 40 percent to 60 percent chance of going to the polls.

Variations in some other provisions also affected turnout. Irregular registration office hours (fewer than forty hours a week) lowered by 2 to 4 percentage points the probability that a person would vote. Offices closed on Saturdays and in the evening decreased by 2 percent to 6 percent the probability of voting. In states that did not allow any form of absentee registration, the chances of voting were 2 percent to 4 percent lower.

We also found that longer voting hours boosted turnout a bit. Keeping the polls open for fourteen hours instead of twelve hours increases from 1 percent to 3 percent the probability that an individual will vote.

Registration Law Reform and Nationwide Turnout

The clearest way to demonstrate the impact of registration provisions on turnout is to show the gap between actual voting rates in 1972 and what these rates would have been if state laws everywhere had been as permissive as they were anywhere. This cannot be learned directly from the probit estimates alone. For example, if a certain provision had a coefficient of −.10 but affected only 15 percent of the population, changing it would not have as much impact on aggregate turnout as would changing a provision that had a coefficient of −.07 but affected half the population.

To estimate the national electoral consequences of changes in the laws, we reweighted the subsample to be a representative sample of the civilian citizen voting-age population, excluding the District of Columbia.[9] Using equation 2 (appendix F), for each respondent we predicted turnout, assuming that certain registration provisions were enacted into law in every state. In each case, the projected provision was the most permissive option already used in some states. In other words, for each provision we assumed that every state had adopted the most permissive registration provision in force in at least one state in 1972. From this estimate we subtracted the predicted turnout, given the provisions as they actually existed in 1972. Summing across respondents yields an estimate of the projected aggregate change in turnout.[10]

Table 4.2 presents these projected increases in turnout for the country as a whole and for various demographic groups. The entries in each column represent the projected increase in turnout for the indicated group if the provision listed at the head of the column were adopted nationwide. The 1972 data do not allow us to estimate directly the increase in turnout that would result from allowing citizens to register *at the polls* on election day or from abolishing registration altogether. The most liberal reforms whose consequences we can estimate can be simulated by setting the registration provisions to the most permissive value existing in 1972. Therefore the "Total" column shows the total projected increase that would result from nationwide adoption of the following provisions:

1. eliminating the closing date;
2. opening registration offices during the forty-hour work week;
3. opening registration offices in the evening and/or on Saturday;
4. permitting absentee registration for the sick, disabled, and absent.

In short, table 4.2 permits us to answer the questions about the impact of registration laws most interesting to policymakers: what will be the consequences, for what groups, of specified changes in the registration laws?

If all states adopted the provisions listed above, turnout would increase by approximately 9.1 percentage points.[11] In 1972, with a national potential electorate of about 134 million, this percentage translates into a projection that an additional 12.2 million people would have voted as a result of the indicated changes in the registration laws. We will decompose this aggregate projection in two ways: (1) to describe those changes that would have the greatest effect and those having relatively little impact and (2) to describe the types of people most affected by the changes.

As we noted above, our findings indicate that relaxing existing provisions in some areas of registration would have no appreciable effect on turnout. In four areas, more permissive provisions would do little to increase voting.

1. *Residency requirements.* In 1972, only two states had effective residency requirements of more than thirty-one days. Tennessee law produced a de facto fifty-day requirement. In Texas, it was sixty-one days. Moreover, the 1970 VRAA required absentee voting in presidential elections for people who had re-

Table 4.2. Projected Increase in Turnout If Registration Laws Were Changed (in Percent)

Percentage increase in turnout if registration laws changed everywhere to:

	Elimination of closing date	Regular office hours	Evening and/or Saturday registration	Some absentee registration	Total increase [a]
National	6.1	.4	2.5	.5	9.1
North	5.6	.2	2.1	.2	7.8
South	7.3	.9	3.6	1.4	12.8
Whites	5.9	.4	2.4	.5	8.9
Blacks	7.2	.5	3.0	.8	11.3
Northern whites	5.5	.2	2.1	.2	7.7
Northern blacks	6.5	.3	2.4	.1	9.1
Southern whites	7.2	.9	3.5	1.3	12.4
Southern blacks	8.2	.8	3.9	1.8	14.5
Years of education					
0–4	8.2	.5	3.3	1.0	13.2
5–7	7.9	.6	3.1	.9	12.6
8	6.9	.4	2.8	.6	10.4
9–11	7.0	.4	2.7	.6	10.4
12	6.1	.4	2.6	.5	9.3
1–3 college	5.4	.3	2.1	.4	7.8
4 college	3.8	.3	1.7	.4	5.6
5+ college	1.9	.1	.9	.1	2.8

Family income					
Under $2,000	7.1	.6	2.9	1.0	11.4
$2,000–$7,499	6.6	.4	2.8	.6	10.1
$7,500–$9,999	6.3	.4	2.6	.5	9.6
$10,000–$14,999	5.8	.4	2.4	.4	8.7
$15,000–$24,999	5.1	.4	2.1	.3	7.4
$25,000+	4.3	.3	1.7	.2	6.2
Age					
18–24	7.2	.4	2.9	.5	11.0
25–31	6.7	.4	2.8	.6	10.2
32–36	6.0	.5	2.5	.5	9.1
37–50	5.5	.4	2.2	.5	8.2
51–69	5.3	.4	2.3	.5	8.1
70–78	6.0	.3	2.1	.5	8.7
79+	6.8	.3	2.9	.5	10.4

[a] The number in this column is the projected increase in turnout if each of the provisions at the head of the first four columns were adopted in all states. The first four columns do not add up to the figure in the total column because the joint effect of a combination of changes is not equal to the arithmetic sum of the individual effects.

cently moved. Every state had adopted such a provision by 1972. The result was that relatively few people were still affected by residency requirements. Our estimates indicate that the probability of voting in the 1972 general election was not affected by existing residency requirements anywhere. Further relaxation of residency requirements would produce no appreciable increase in voting. This represents a substantial shift from conclusions about the effect of residency requirements in 1960 and doubtless reflects the enormous legal changes since then. Present requirements, in combination with provisions for absentee voting by new residents, have made residency requirements relatively unobtrusive.

2. *Deputy registrars.* With other variables controlled, people in states that authorize deputy registrars are no likelier to vote. Authorizing the appointment of deputy registrars in every state would not have an appreciable effect on turnout.

3. *Where to register.* The location of the registrar's office does not affect the probability that people will vote. Being able to register in one's neighborhood as opposed to going to a municipal or county office does not increase turnout.

4. *Years before purging.* Periodic purging from the registration rolls of those who did not vote in the previous election does not decrease the likelihood that otherwise eligible citizens will go to the polls. Allowing a citizen who fails to vote to remain on the rolls for eight years does not increase voter turnout above what it would be if he were purged from the rolls for failure to vote in a single election.

Changes in four other areas of registration laws would increase turnout, although in only one respect—the closing date—would the change be substantial.

1. *Absentee registration.* Ten states did not permit civilian absentee registration. This restriction affects the sick and disabled, as well as people who are away from home because of business, school, or vacations. Allowing civilian absentee registration for these groups will increase national turnout by about .5 percent. Nearly all of this increase would occur in the South.

Five states had universal civilian absentee registration, permitting anyone to register by mail, not just the absent, disabled, and sick. This plan received considerable attention in 1976 as Congress debated nationwide postcard registration. The House passed a bill for postcard registration, but only after amending it so that the government lacked authority to mail the cards to every household. Thus the burden of obtaining the postcard was left on the individual, although presumably civic and political groups could distribute the cards. The House bill was similar to the system used by five states in 1972. Our estimates indicate that in 1972 this type of registration system did *not* result in higher turnout than the more limited absentee registration discussed in the preceding paragraph. Therefore it appears that this plan would not have much effect. The crucial amendment to the House bill shifted the initiative from the government to the individual. Our data do not permit us to estimate the impact of a scheme that, like the original bill, relieves the individual of the burden of initiating registration proceedings; no state did this.

2. *Irregular weekday office hours.* Although the location of the registrar's office does not affect the level of voter turnout, its hours do. Residents of states where registration offices are not regularly open during normal business hours are less likely to vote than are people in states where one can register any time during the business week. Allowing registration at any time during the work week would increase national turnout by about .4 percentage points. Turnout in the South would increase by .9 percent, compared to .2 percentage points in the North.

3. *Evening and Saturday registration.* People living in states where registration offices are required to remain open beyond normal business hours are more likely to vote than are residents of states where offices need not be open in the evening or on Saturday. Requiring evening and/or Saturday registration everywhere in the country would raise turnout by 2.5 percent. This change would have more impact in the South. An additional 3.9 percent of Southern blacks and 3.5 percent of Southern whites would go to the polls. The comparable figures for the North are 2.4 percent and 2.1 percent.

4. *Closing date.* Of the legal changes considered here, the one

that would have the greatest impact on turnout would be elimination of the closing date. An early closing date decreases the probability of voting. If one could register until election day itself, when media coverage is widest and interest is greatest, turnout would increase by about 6.1 percentage points. This change would have meant an additional 8 million voters in 1972. If the closing date had been a week before the election everywhere in the country, turnout in 1972 would have been 4.5 percent higher. Because of the earlier closing dates in the South, people living there would be affected more than Northerners by such changes.

Our projections indicate that if all the changes summarized in table 4.2 had been instituted throughout the country in 1972, turnout in the presidential election that year would have been 9.1 percent higher. This represents 12.2 million additional people who would have voted if the registration laws everywhere had been as lenient as in the most permissive states. (With a seven-day closing date, the total increase in turnout would have been 7.7 percent.)

Variations in the Effect of Registration Laws

We have already seen that the effect of relaxing registration laws would not be felt evenly across the population. One reason, of course, is that the gap between the status quo and uniformly permissive provisions is much greater in some places than in others. In 1972, few states came close to the hypothetical permissive situation assumed in table 4.2.[12] The laws in the Southern states would undergo the biggest change. Therefore, making registration easier would have the greatest impact in that part of the country. If all four provisions described in table 4.2 were enacted, turnout in the South would increase by approximately 12.8 percentage points, while turnout in the North would go up by about 7.8 percent. This difference between the regions is caused by two factors. First, the Southern states at present have more restrictive statutes than the rest of the country. Easing the laws would thus cause greater changes in the South. Second, since people with fewer years of formal education would benefit most from the changes, and since the South has a lower mean level of education than the Northern states, a greater percentage of Southerners would benefit from the changes.

Within the South, the projected increases in turnout for blacks and whites are relatively similar. Turnout among whites would increase 12.4 percent, while black turnout in the South would go up by 14.5 percentage points. In the North, where the gap between the races in educational attainment is smaller, there is less racial difference in projected turnout. An additional 7.7 percent of Northern whites would go to the polls, as compared with a gain in turnout of 9.1 percent for blacks.

The most striking variations in the effects of registration reform would be among people at different levels of education.[13] Liberalizing registration provisions would have by far the greatest impact on the least educated and relatively little effect on well-educated people. Turnout would increase by 13.2 percent among people with fewer than five years of school, by 10.4 percent among elementary-school graduates, by 9.3 percent among those with a high school diploma, and by only 2.8 percent among people with some postgraduate schooling.

These findings fit predictions based on our theory of turnout: the appeal of voting increases with education, and the costs of voting vary inversely with education. It is not surprising, then, that apparently trivial additions to the burden of registering raise the cost of voting above the threshold of many people. We see that threshold as set by two factors: the individual's interest in the election and his ability to manage the procedural steps required to cast a ballot.

Formal education increases one's capacity for understanding and working with complex, abstract, and intangible subjects —that is, subjects like politics. Acquisition of these skills and facts heightens interest in politics. Schooling also imparts experience with bureaucratic relationships and such simple information-seeking skills as looking up a necessary item in a book.

Regardless of one's degree of political interest, this heightened level of understanding and information would also reduce the costs of registering, even in the most restrictive state. In short, education is likely to increase interest in politics and to reduce the costs of manifesting that interest by voting.

The more permissive the registration laws, the lower the time, energy, and information costs of voting. This is of greatest benefit to people whose interest is not sufficient to carry them across the higher threshold imposed by more restrictive provisions. The costs imposed by restrictive laws might be trifling to an educated person and increasingly daunting to those with little schooling.

Thus for someone who is interested in politics, who can anticipate the need for registration before the peak excitement of election eve, and who can easily locate the registrar's office, registration is a relatively costless act. On the other hand, for someone whose interest is aroused only a few days before the election, who has minimal exposure to information, and who is less adept at learning things like places and hours of registration, the whole process is a much more difficult hurdle. The barriers imposed by restrictive laws seem to make little difference to the well educated but are a fairly formidable impediment to people with less interest and bureaucratic skill. To put it another way, the difference in turnout produced by variations in registration laws is an indication of the varying commitment and capacity to vote of different kinds of people.

The Political Consequences of Registration Law Reform

Liberalizing the registration laws would expand the electorate and increase disproportionately the turnout of poor people. Most scholars, journalists, and politicians have assumed that easier registration would markedly change the social class composition of the electorate. The result would be a less interested and informed voting population, a windfall of votes for the Democratic party, and more support for social welfare policies (Polsby and Wildavsky 1976, p. 129).[14] The Left views the prospect this way:

It is more likely they [nonvoters] would line up behind programs and candidates that would improve and expand the
welfare state, end poverty, and bring forth a greater measure of social justice and economic security for the common
citizen. . . . So it is those on the bottom of the social order
who stand to gain the most from an expansion of the popular
base of political participation. [Amundsen 1977, pp. 136–37]

Commenting on President Carter's election day registration
plan, the conservative columnist James Kilpatrick seemed to
agree:

The thinly disguised ulterior motive [for Carter's proposal],
freely if privately conceded on Capitol Hill, is to benefit the
Democratic party. This is a political power play, as brazen as
any stunt ever pulled in the bad old days of Tammany Hall.
. . . [San Francisco Chronicle, May 16, 1977, p. 38]

It seems safe to conclude that these fears help explain Republican
and Southern Democratic opposition to legislative proposals for
making registration easier.[15]

Such beliefs are based in part on the common assumption that
anything that expands the electorate is good for Democratic candidates and liberal causes. The empirical foundation is the well-
known fact that poor people have lower turnout rates. It would
seem that the findings we have just presented about the greater
impact of registration laws on the uneducated would confirm the
conventional wisdom, encourage Democratic politicians to make
the laws more permissive, and reinforce conservative opposition
to this step. This conclusion is wrong, however, because it in-
volves an understandable confusion between two sorts of statistics. What is overlooked is the elementary (if not obvious) point
that the politically significant facts are not rates of change but
whether the expanded voting population resulting from registration law reform would be different in politically important ways
from the less numerous actual voters.

We used equation 2 to project what the demographic, partisan, and ideological characteristics of the voters would have been
in 1972 if the registration provisions assumed in table 4.2 were

instituted nationally. We compared these projections to the characteristics of the actual voters in order to estimate how the voting population would change as a result of making registration easier.[16] The demographic comparisons, based on our original census sample, are summarized in table 4.3. Tables 4.4 and 4.5 compare the two groups with respect to party identification and attitudes on several issues, based on data from the 1972 Michigan National Election Study. All three tables lead to the same conclusion: the expanded voting population produced by relaxing registration laws would be remarkably similar to the actual voters.

The largest increases would occur in demographic categories. With more permissive registration laws, the voting population would include slightly bigger proportions of groups that are traditionally light voters. The change, such as it is, would be greatest in the South. In 1972 people who had not graduated from high school comprised 29.7 percent of all voters. Relaxing registration provisions would have increased their share by 1.6 percent. In the North, this category would have accounted for an additional 1.2 percent of the voting population. In the South, the increase would be 2.7 percent. *This latter figure is the largest shift in the composition of the voting population that we could find in any descriptive category.* College-educated people would account for a correspondingly smaller share of all voters, down from 31.9 percent to 30.6 percent in the North, from 32.2 percent to 29.7 percent in the South, and from 32.0 percent to 30.5 percent in the country as a whole.

Differences in income are generally more important to political choice than are educational cleavages, and here the impact of registration reform would be even smaller. The proportion of all voters comprised of people with annual family incomes of less than $10,000 would increase by 1.3 percent. The gain would be .8 percent in the North and 1.4 percent in the South.

Projected changes in racial composition would be smaller still. Nonwhites would comprise an additional .3 percent of the national voting population. The increase would be .2 percent in the North and .9 percent in the South.

Finally, the proportion of voters comprised of people under the age of thirty-two would increase from 28.3 percent to 29.5 percent. The increase would be 1.1 percent in the North and 1.7 percent in the South.

In sum, although making it easier for people to register would increase turnout, it would have a very small impact on the demographic characteristics of voters. Voters in the aggregate would be marginally less educated, poorer, blacker, and younger. These changes would be somewhat greater in the South.

Some people have speculated that if a bigger share of the voters were young, poor, and uneducated, voters would be substantially less interested in politics (Key 1964, p. 590; Polsby and Wildavsky 1976, pp. 239–41). As one might suspect from the demographic projections we have just summarized, changes in this regard would be very modest.[17] Liberalizing registration laws would increase by .6 percent the proportion of voters who have hardly any interest in the campaign. An additional .8 percent would be comprised of those who follow politics only now and then or hardly at all. Voters' level of attentiveness to politics would not be significantly altered by relaxing voter registration laws.

These findings about the minimal changes in the demographic composition of voters are inconsistent with the general belief that easier registration laws would be a major boon for Democrats. Our projection, in table 4.4, confirms doubts about the validity of the conventional wisdom. The partisan characteristics of the hypothetical voters would be virtually identical to those of the actual voters. In 1972, 36.4 percent of those voting were aligned with the Republican party as outright identifiers or as Independents who said they were "closer to" Republicans. With more liberal registration laws, Republicans would comprise 35.9 percent of voters—a wholly insignificant shift. The Democratic windfall would be equally trivial—a gain of .3 percent (three-tenths of a percentage point).[18]

Presidential elections have been decided by tiny margins, and an apparently insignificant advantage for one party might turn

Table 4.3. Composition of the Actual 1972 Voters and of the Projected Voters after Relaxation of Registration Laws

	Northern voters		Southern voters		Total voters	
	Actual	Projected	Actual	Projected	Actual	Projected
Years of education						
0–4	1.4%	1.6%	3.9%	4.6%	2.0%	2.4%
5–7	3.7	4.0	6.9	7.8	4.4	4.9
8	9.6	9.9	6.1	6.5	8.8	9.1
9–11	14.5	14.9	14.3	15.0	14.5	14.9
12	38.9	39.0	36.5	36.5	38.4	38.3
1–3 college	16.8	16.4	15.2	14.6	16.4	16.0
4 college	8.4	8.0	10.5	9.5	8.9	8.4
5+ college	6.7	6.2	6.5	5.6	6.7	6.1
Total	100.0%	100.0%	99.9%	100.1%	100.1%	100.1%
Family income						
Under $2,000	4.2%	4.4%	7.7%	8.1%	5.0%	5.3%
$2,000–$7,499	28.9	29.4	35.9	37.0	30.5	31.3
$7,500–$9,999	14.5	14.6	13.0	13.2	14.1	14.3
$10,000–$14,999	28.7	28.6	23.8	23.2	27.6	27.3
$15,000–$24,999	18.0	17.6	15.4	14.5	17.4	16.8
$25,000+	5.7	5.5	4.3	3.9	5.4	5.1
Total	100.0%	100.0%	100.1%	99.9%	100.0%	100.1%
Race						
Whites	92.5%	92.3%	87.2%	86.3%	91.3%	90.8%
Nonwhites	7.5	7.7	12.8	13.7	8.7	9.1
Total	100.0%	100.0%	100.0%	100.0%	100.0%	99.9%
Age						
18–24	14.6%	15.4%	12.5%	13.9%	14.1%	15.0%
25–31	13.9	14.1	15.4	15.7	14.2	14.5
32–36	9.0	8.9	9.5	9.4	9.1	9.1
37–50	25.5	24.9	26.5	25.6	25.7	25.1
51–69	28.1	27.6	27.3	26.6	28.0	27.3
70–78	6.7	6.7	5.7	5.7	6.5	6.4
79+	2.3	2.4	3.0	3.1	2.4	2.5
Total	100.1%	100.0%	99.9%	100.0%	100.0%	99.9%

Table 4.4. Partisan Composition of Actual and Projected Voters in 1972

Party identification	Voters	
	Actual	Projected
Strong Democrat	14.6%	14.7%
Weak Democrat	25.3	25.5
Independent Democrat	11.2	11.2
Independent	12.4	12.6
Independent Republican	10.9	10.9
Weak Republican	14.2	14.0
Strong Republican	11.3	11.0
Total	99.9%	99.9%
(N)	(1,809)	(2,044)

Source: Authors' analysis of data from Center for Political Studies 1972 National Election Study.

out to be the difference between victory and defeat (O'Rourke 1978). Nevertheless, we consider the partisan consequences of registration law reform to be trivial. First, in contrast to the common belief that election day registration would produce a Democratic bonanza, a .3 percent gain for the Democrats is quite insignificant. Second, when based on a survey sample, a difference of .3 percent cannot be distinguished statistically from zero. Our hypothetical expanded electorate consists of 2,044 cases in the Michigan sample. A difference of .3 (actually, .279) percent reflects just six cases. It would be foolhardy to base predictions about the real world on a shift of six respondents. The sampling error alone is many times greater than .3 percent.

Assessing the possibility that presidential election outcomes might be affected requires a look at individual state results, not the meaningless national popular vote. We lack the data for a simulation of each state's electorate, but we can produce a reasonably serviceable substitute. This can be done by assuming for the moment that the tiny changes in the Michigan sample will occur in the real world and that in each state the voters will be .279 percent more Democratic and .200 percent more pure Independent. Furthermore, let us assume that in any given election, 80 percent of the Democrats and 50 percent of the Independents will vote for the Democratic presidential candidate. On average, then, .323 percentage points will be added to the Democratic vote in each state [.8(.279) + .5(.200)]. How many states that voted Republican in recent elections would have gone Democratic if .323 percentage points had been taken from the Republicans and added to the Democratic vote total? Of the 200 state contests between 1964 and 1976, only 1 (1976) would have turned out differently. Between 1948 and 1960 only 3 of 194 state decisions would have changed (1 each in 1952, 1956, and 1960). In no election would the national outcome have been different.

Of course, a future presidential election *could* be decided by a shift of .323 percent. As we have tried to show, however, this is not very probable. The more important point is that with survey samples, a difference of .3 percent is statistically equivalent to zero.

Although the partisan balance would not be affected by registration reform, is it possible that these changes could increase the voting strength of people with particular attitude configurations? It has been suggested, for example, that this would result in more ballot strength for people who are liberal on economic issues but conservative on social and racial issues. Comparing the actual and hypothetical voters on a number of issue attitudes measured in the 1972 Michigan study, we found traces of this pattern, but the differences were inconsistent and invariably tiny. All such differences were far smaller than sampling error, which leads us to warn that they may well not reflect any difference in the real world. Some comparisons of attitude distributions among actual and projected voters are presented in table 4.5. This table reports the *largest* differences we found on issues.

If the voting population were expanded through more permissive registration, the proportion of voters who say that the federal government should see that everyone has a job and an adequate standard of living would increase by .3 percentage points. Support for government-sponsored health insurance would increase by .1 percent. The effect of registration reform on voters' support for social welfare issues, in short, would be negligible.

Table 4.5. Attitudes of Actual and Projected Voters in 1972

	Voters	
	Actual	Projected
Government should see that everyone has a job and a good standard of living	30.4%	30.7%
Middle of the road	23.9	23.7
People should get ahead on their own	45.7	45.6
Total	100.0%	100.0%
Federal government should ensure school integration	44.7%	44.0%
Government should stay out of this issue	55.3	56.0
Total	100.0%	100.0%
Legalize marijuana	22.7%	22.3%
Middle of the road	11.3	11.1
Increase penalties for use	66.0	66.6
Total	100.0%	100.0%
Women deserve equal role in business and government	50.5%	49.7%
Middle of the road	20.8	20.7
Women's place is in the home	29.2	29.6
Total	100.0%	100.0%
Self-described liberals	25.8%	25.8%
Moderates	36.2	36.5
Conservatives	38.0	37.7
Total	100.0%	100.0%

Source: Authors' analysis of data from Center for Political Studies 1972 National Election Study.

Virtually the same can be said of other issue areas. The expanded electorate would include .7 percent more people who think that the federal government should shun involvement in school integration and .3 percent more opponents of school busing. The picture is the same on "social" issues. Support for the proposition that woman's place is in the home would increase by half a percentage point. Opponents of legalized marijuana would make up an additional .6 percent. The proportion of voters who call themselves liberals would remain unchanged. In short, the ideological composition of the voters would be virtually identical.

In summary, registration substantially raises the costs of voting. The greater the obstacles to voting, the more difficult it is for a citizen to ensure his eligibility and the less likely it is that he will vote. Four registration provisions were found to present significant barriers to citizens voting: early closing dates, irregular office hours, no Saturday or evening registration, and no absentee registration. The costs of registering do not fall equally on everyone. Those with the least education—who are least able to cope with the bureaucratic hurdles of registration—are most affected by these provisions.

If every state had had registration laws in 1972 as permissive as those in the most permissive states, turnout would have been about 9 percentage points higher in the presidential election. The political consequences of these reforms are measured by comparing actual voters to the larger number of hypothetical voters estimated by projecting rates of change in turnout. This comparison shows that relaxing registration requirements would produce a voting population very similar to the actual 1972 voters. The number of voters would increase, but there would be virtually no change in their demographic, partisan, or ideological characteristics. They would be more numerous, but not different.

The changes we have considered are within a narrow compass of alternatives. One question that remains is how much national voter turnout would increase if the burden for registration shifted from the individual to the government. What would be the increase in turnout if, as in most democracies, the government took the initiative for registering voters by establishing national voter lists through a door-to-door canvass or by mailing postcards to all citizens? Our data do not allow us to make a precise estimate of the impact of a registration system in which the government bears the responsibility for establishing voter eligibility and where virtually all the costs of registering are removed from the individual. Given the results that would be achieved by the relatively minor changes discussed above, we are confident that establishing a European type of registration system would increase voter turnout by substantially more than 9 percent.

5: POLITICAL STAKES
AND POLITICAL CULTURE

To this point we have assumed that the citizen's political involvement is invariably avocational and that the individual benefits of the voting act are purely symbolic: a sense of citizen duty fulfilled or a political preference or group loyalty expressed. These assumptions are not valid for many people who work for the government and deal with the subject matter of politics on the job. Moreover, some government employees have very concrete motivations for going to the polls: if they fail to vote, they may lose their jobs, damage their chances of promotion, or incur the disfavor of their superiors. If the opposition wins, some patronage employees will be out of jobs. For such people, politics is far from intangible, distant, and abstract.

Mentioning this style of politics leads us to note that so far we have said little about the effect on turnout of "political culture" or "political environment." One aspect of political culture distinguishes between places where machine politics is important and those states where patronage is scanty and merit considerations govern public personnel practices. Is turnout higher where patronage is dominant? Or are high voting rates associated with the high-minded approach to government found in states that shun machine politics? Another area of inquiry about political culture is the South, traditionally America's "different" region. Students of voting have noted the lower voting rates in the South (Flanigan and Zingale 1975, pp. 26–27). Is this an artifact of the region's lower educational levels and its higher black population, or is low turnout a more general Southern characteristic? In order to analyze Southern voting rates, we must, of course, also consider the turnout of ethnic minorities. We begin with this latter topic, and then proceed to consider the South and variations in turnout associated with machine and reformed politics.

Blacks

In the aggregate, blacks are less likely to vote than whites. One historical reason was widespread disenfranchisement in the South, where blacks are a much larger proportion of the population than in the rest of the country. In 1962 only 5 percent of the black voting-age population in Mississippi and only 13 percent in Alabama were registered. The Voting Rights Act of 1965 provided for replacement of local election officials by federal registrars in many Southern states. The result was a sharp increase in black electoral participation.

Black turnout is still substantially lower than that of whites, however, in both the North and the South. Forty-nine percent of Southern blacks voted in 1972, compared to 58 percent of Southern whites. In the rest of the country, the figures were 61 percent and 71 percent. Since blacks are considerably younger and less educated than whites, we would expect them to vote less. A correct estimate of the relationship between race and turnout requires that socioeconomic differences between the races be held constant. We found that once this was done, there was no evidence of lingering illegal disenfranchisement in the South and, as we observed in the previous chapter, no signs that blacks were more affected by the South's generally more restrictive registration laws. Our multivariate analysis for the 1972 election also showed that blacks voted at a *slightly higher* rate than whites. The marginal impact of race was highest among the least educated. Compared to their white counterparts, blacks who had not attended college had a 4 percent higher probability of voting. This racial difference diminished as education increased, to the point where there was no difference at the postgraduate level. Other scholars also report higher turnout for blacks, once demographic variables have been controlled (Olsen 1970; Verba and

Nie 1972, pp. 170–71).[1] This has been attributed to blacks' sense of racial identity (Verba and Nie 1972, pp. 152–55) and to their greater community consciousness (Olsen 1970, p. 684).

Our probit analysis of 1974 data showed blacks voting at the same rate as whites, with other variables held constant. We are reluctant to conclude from our contrast of 1972 and 1974 findings that the relationship between race and turnout is greater in presidential elections because of a presidential contest's higher stimulus to blacks. When the positive effect of race has been reported, it is always quite small. It is reasonable to expect, then, that in at least some samples the estimated relationship of race to turnout will be indistinguishable from zero.[2] Thus *if* blacks vote more than whites (once the demographic differences between the groups have been accounted for), the difference in turnout is probably very small.

Hispanics

Little research has been done on the political behavior of Hispanic-Americans, of whom Chicanos and Puerto Ricans are the most numerous. These groups are represented by only a handful of respondents in the standard national survey sample. For example, the 1974 Michigan National Election Study reported turnout for just thirteen Chicanos and a lone Puerto Rican. Spanish origin was ascertained in the 1974 census study, but not in the one conducted in 1972. The 1974 Current Population Survey included 2,553 Chicanos and 807 Puerto Ricans for whom turnout was reported. We oversampled both groups in our subsampling procedure, and our probit estimates are based on 335 Chicanos and 236 Puerto Ricans.

Only 32 percent of Chicanos and 27 percent of Puerto Ricans voted in 1974, compared to 37 percent of blacks and 50 percent of non-Hispanic whites. Journalistic accounts provide a number of speculations about the reasons for this low voting rate. According to the *New York Times* (1979, p. 16), it is a result of the language barrier and "a general cultural estrangement from the white mainstream." Another source suggests that sluggish turnout among Chicanos may be due to

> the lack of a two-party tradition in Mexico, the fear of revealing "undocumented" (illegal) household members, and the fact that so many Mexican-Americans with long histories as migrant workers have never had a chance to establish voting residencies. [Peirce and Hagstrom 1979, p. 550]

As we will see, these elaborate speculations are unnecessary to explain the turnout of Hispanic-Americans.

First, we will examine Chicano turnout. Contrary to the popular view, only 5 percent of Chicanos are farm laborers. Chicanos are like most other Hispanic groups in that they are predominantly urban, young, and uneducated.[3] Once these and other demographic factors have been held constant, we find that Chicanos are 3 percent *more* likely to vote than the rest of the population. We are cautious about making too much of this estimate, since the number is both substantively and statistically close to zero. Perhaps the safest conclusion is that Chicanos vote at about the same rate as the rest of the population.[4]

Like Chicanos, Puerto Ricans are less educated, poorer, and younger than the majority population. The similarities end there, however. Sixty percent of the Puerto Ricans lived in one state (New York) in 1974, while 75 percent of the Chicanos lived in Texas and California. Chicanos who enter this country legally must wait a minimum of five years before gaining citizenship and thus eligibility to vote, while Puerto Ricans are already citizens and are thus automatically eligible to vote as soon as they have established residence in one of the fifty states. Chicanos must of necessity go through at least five years of acculturation in the course of attaining citizenship and must learn the rudimentary norms of participation and citizen duty. Because their homeland is so close and travel across the border is so easy, Mexicans find it easier than do immigrants from almost any other country to combine maintenance of ties to the old country with achievement of whatever goals brought them to the United States. Leonel J. Castillo, the Chicano ex-chief of the Immigration and Naturalization Service, observed:

> Mexicans historically have been one of the slowest groups to naturalize. Many don't ever become citizens because of the proximity of Mexico and the pride that says they want to die in Mexico. [quoted in Peirce and Hagstrom 1979, p. 550]

We expect that Mexican immigrants who become citizens despite these sentimental considerations are particularly likely to have the sort of civic-minded feeling that might lead them to the polling place.

The opposite is true of Puerto Ricans. They are potential voters as soon as they set foot on mainland soil, although many are temporary visitors, and others think of themselves this way even after years of residence here. With this in mind, we might expect that turnout among Puerto Ricans would be lower than among Chicanos and the rest of the population. And in fact this is the case: with other demographic variables held constant, Puerto Ricans were about 7 percent less likely to vote in 1974.[5]

The South

For generations Southern voting rates were far below those in the rest of the country. Some of the reasons were the poll tax, the lack of two-party competition, and widespread disenfranchisement of blacks. As these practices faded into the past during the 1960s, turnout increased in the South at the same time that it fell elsewhere. Even so, a considerable gap remains; 57 percent of Southern citizens voted in 1972, as compared with 70 percent of Northerners.

The regional turnout disparity is greatest among the less educated. Southerners with eight years of schooling vote 16 percentage points less than their Northern counterparts. The regional turnout deficit for people with postgraduate training is less than 3 percent. As these findings indicate, only some of Southerners' lower turnout is explained by their generally lower educational attainment. By the same token, the South's more demanding registration laws do not fully account for the lower voting rates. In fact, when all variables have been held constant, turnout among Southerners is still 6 percent less than among Americans in other regions.

Lacking any other clue, we think this might reflect a sort of regional memory, a vestigial effect from the days when both law and custom discouraged participation. This political culture is generally considered an outgrowth of the traditional Southern preoccupation with excluding blacks from political power. Although the specific institutional manifestations of this era have faded, the spirit may linger on. If there is any merit in this explanation, we would expect it to apply most strongly to older Southerners, socialized in the days before the rise of Republicanism, racial equality, and migration from the North. This is just what we find. Among people aged eighteen to thirty-one, Southerners are only 3 percent less likely to vote than their Northern counterparts. The regional gap is 6 percent for those aged thirty-two to sixty-nine, 8 percent for people seventy to seventy-eight years old, and 9 percent for people seventy-nine and older. It looks as if history is on the side of rising turnout in the South.

One dynamic factor contributing to this trend is the growing influx of Yankees. Younger, richer, and better educated, these transplanted Northerners are more likely to vote than the natives. They comprised fully 25 percent of the Southern voting population in 1976, as compared with a mere 7 percent in 1952 (Wolfinger and Arseneau 1978, pp. 188, 192–95). This suggests that in turnout, as in so many other areas of political life, the South is likely to lose most of its distinctive character in the coming generation. Nevertheless, the persistence of the regional gap that we have reported testifies to the durability of the regional political culture.

Government Employees

People differ in their ability to discern how their interests will be affected by one candidate's victory over the other. They also differ in the extent of their actual vulnerability to electoral outcomes. While we all are presumably affected by the difference between what one candidate and the other would actually do while in office, some people are more likely to be helped or hurt by a particular outcome. This is most obviously true of public officials who serve at the pleasure of the relevant president, governor, or mayor. It is less clearly the case with other public servants whose jobs increase their sensitivity to the stakes of an election.

Thus government employees, like farmers, are another group that is likely to perceive the relative immediacy of an election. While farmers comprise less than 3 percent of the labor force, *one of every six* people employed in 1972 worked for the government. Public employees are perhaps the fastest growing segment of the labor force. In 1960 there were 8.8 million employees at all levels of government. This number grew to 13 million in 1970 and to 15 million in 1976. The increase is almost entirely at the state and local levels; the number of federal employees has scarcely changed for more than a decade.

Public employees vote at a very high rate. In 1972, 83 percent of them went to the polls, as compared with 65 percent of the rest of the sample. This might be nothing more than an artifact of other demographic characteristics. In the first place, government workers are better educated; 49 percent went to college, more than double the proportion in the rest of the population. Second, almost 70 percent have white-collar jobs, mostly professional, technical, and clerical. Their income, however, differs in more complex ways. They tend to be better paid at the lower occupational levels and worse off at the higher reaches. As usual, this is a case for multivariate analysis, which confirms that public employment does indeed give a substantial boost to turnout, particularly for the less educated. Before examining this finding in detail, it might be useful to consider more fully different reasons why government employment would lead to higher turnout.

Due to the nature of their work, many public employees are more concerned about the outcome of elections. Many deal on a daily basis with subjects that become campaign issues or would be affected by election outcomes. Of course, some public servants find no political relevance in their jobs. The experiences of a file clerk in the Social Security Administration, for example, are probably identical to those of his counterpart in an insurance agency. Even where the work is identical, however, a shift of employer might alter one's level of political consciousness. This certainly happens when, for example, a professor moves from a private to a public university. In the aggregate, then, public employees are more acquainted with and interested in political issues; thus they are more likely to vote.

There is a completely different line of argument about the motivations of those state and local government employees who owe their positions to political sponsors. They have an undeniable and crucial stake in the election. If the wrong candidate wins, they will be out of a job, demoted, or transferred to the local equivalent of Siberia. In Pennsylvania, for example, a newly elected governor can replace about 50,000 state employees; the chief executives of Illinois, Indiana, New York, and some other states are not far behind (Tolchin and Tolchin 1972, p. 96). This provides a very strong incentive to vote, even if one is completely persuaded that a single ballot can never be decisive. Moreover, patronage employees may not be free agents when it comes to voting. Political machines often coerce their members to vote and keep records of their performance, even when the crucial local or state offices are not at issue (Wolfinger 1974, pp. 74-83). In these cases there is a stake not just in the outcome but in the act of voting itself.

Thus we have two explanations for government employees' high turnout: (1) a "political alertness" hypothesis, which would be supported by a finding of higher turnout by public employees in all states and (2) a "patronage hypothesis," which would be validated if turnout were particularly high among state and local employees where patronage, not the merit system, is an important path to getting and keeping government jobs. Unfortunately, we do not have a single data set that combines all the information needed to test these hypotheses. Our 1972 data permit us to identify each respondent's state of residence but do not distinguish among federal, state, and local employees. Because federal employees are included, we have an imprecise measure of possible variations in turnout from one political culture to another. This gives a conservative bias to our findings, since it produces an underestimation of the effect of patronage considerations on turnout. The 1974 data set has the opposite problem; only twelve large states are identified, but many public employees are classified by level of government. The clearest strategy is to present our findings for each year in turn.

Our classification of states was devised in the following way. We removed the eleven Southern states from consideration and from the remainder chose ten states in which machine politics was important and ten more where the merit system seemed supreme in both state and local government personnel practices. We based our choices on our reading in scholarly and journalistic sources. Conceding the impressionistic nature of this process, we think it would be difficult to compile a list of machine politics states that did not include our ten: Illinois, Indiana, Maryland, Massachusetts, Missouri, New Jersey, New York, Pennsylvania, Rhode Island, and West Virginia. By the same token, anyone's list of states at the opposite end of the spectrum would resemble our "reform" states: California, Idaho, Minnesota, Nebraska, North Dakota, Oregon, South Dakota, Utah, Washington, and Wisconsin.[6] We found that voting rates of government employees in the reform states did not differ from those in the remaining nineteen Northern states. We combined these groups, thus producing three categories of states for our analysis of turnout by government employees: eleven Southern states, ten Northern patronage states, and the remaining twenty-nine Northern states. The results of our analysis are presented in Table 5.1.

As Table 5.1 shows, both hypotheses about high turnout among government workers are supported by the data, although the evidence for the patronage hypothesis is much more striking. In all three categories of states, when other demographic variables are controlled, government employees vote at a higher rate than private employees. The difference is largest at the lower educational levels and virtually disappears for those with postgrad-

Table 5.1.   Turnout of Government Employees by Education,
Region, and Political Culture, in 1972 (in Percent)

Years of education	Increase in turnout of government employees over all other workers		
	Patronage states	Other Northern states	Southern states
0–8 (grammar school)	18	5	5
9–12 (high school)	14	4	5
1–3 college	4	4	4
4 college	3	3	4
5+ college	1	1	2
Total	9	3	4

Note: The entry in each cell is the probit estimate (see appendix C) of the difference between the turnout of government employees and of all other workers in the indicated category of education and state. For example, Southern public employees with a grammar-school education have a turnout rate 5 percentage points higher than do Southern private employees with the same amount of education.

uate experience. This suggests that working for the government is for some people a "substitute" for formal schooling—a way to acquire interests and norms that ordinarily are a product of college attendance.

The increase in turnout of government workers in Southern and nonpatronage Northern states is dwarfed by the corresponding increment for public employees in the ten patronage states. In the other forty states, government workers who have not been to college vote about 5 percentage points more than private workers at the same levels of schooling. In the patronage states, on the other hand, the gap is 18 percent for those who have not been to high school and 14 percent for workers who have gone to high school but not to college. Government workers in patronage states with less than nine years of education are 13 percent more likely to vote than public employees with the same amount of schooling in the other forty states. Those with a high school education are 10 percent more likely to vote than their public employee counterparts elsewhere. There is no difference at all among public employees who have been to college.

These differences between the higher turnout of public employees in the patronage states and in the rest of the country are a measure of the impact on turnout of patronage considerations. Our findings are consistent with the proposition that patronage jobs are particularly important to the working class (Wolfinger 1974, pp. 92–99). Better educated government workers are less vulnerable to such pressures. Teachers, the largest group of public employees, are often protected both by tenure and union contracts and thus are relatively immune to political threats.

If the high turnout of public employees in patronage states can be explained by the higher political stakes in those states, we should expect to find a higher voting rate in such states among the mass public as well. After all, the pressure on the patronage employee is not just to go to the polls himself but also to turn out the vote in his precinct. Comparing all ten patronage states to the rest of the North, we found vitually no difference.[7]

The picture changed when we confined our examination to states with gubernatorial elections in 1972. Among this group, turnout was significantly higher in the patronage states. As we might expect, the increase was greatest among the least educated. Residents of patronage states with a grammar-school education were 6 percent more likely to vote than were their counterparts in the other Northern states. People who had not gone beyond high school were 6 percent likelier to vote, while those who had attended college were between 2 percent and 5 percent more likely to go to the polls. We would not expect most political machines to work very hard to get out the vote for George McGovern. But we would expect efforts to get out the vote if the governor's chair were at stake. In an earlier study (Rosenstone and Wolfinger 1978, p. 31) we found that a concurrent gubernatorial election increased the probability of turnout from 1 percent to 2 percent. Our present analysis reveals that this effect is confined to the patronage states; elsewhere in 1972, there was no increase in turnout in the presence of a gubernatorial election. The effect on turnout of the concurrent election, then, would seem to reflect patronage-motivated electioneering, not the increment contributed by voters interested only in the race for the governor's mansion.

At the other end of the spectrum from the patronage states are our ten "reform" states, noted for their high levels of civic virtue, abhorrence of machine politics, and so on. Turnout in this latter group was 5 percent higher than in the patronage states. This difference can be explained entirely by the higher levels of education and less restrictive registration laws in the reform states. Each of the propositions about government employees and mass publics in the patronage states was tested also for the reform states. In no respect was turnout of the masses[8] or government employees[9] in the reform states different from those in any other category of states.

These findings about turnout in reform states are inconsistent with the notion that the states' political culture is a determinant of the amount of citizen participation at the polls. Our reform states have been designated by Daniel Elazar (1972, chapter 4) as having "individualistic" or "moralistic" political cultures. These attributes have been advanced as causes of higher rates of voting (Sharkansky 1969; Johnson 1976). We could find no evidence for this position. Once region, registration laws, and educational level are held constant, turnout in the reform states does not differ from that elsewhere. If their political culture does affect turnout, the relationship is expressed entirely through the impact of their voter registration laws.

The available variables for our 1974 data allow us to identify public school teachers (15 percent of all government employees) and the level of government of all members of the labor force whose detailed job category is "public administration." This includes nearly all federal employees and about one-fourth of state and local workers. Thus in 1974 we cannot identify those public employees whose duties are not essentially governmental, such as bus drivers, custodians, machinists. They are included in the private employee category.

Using these data the effect on turnout of being a government employee is summarized in table 5.2. These estimates are consistent with the argument and data presented above. Federal employees and teachers, who are assumed to be virtually unaffected by patronage, vote about 4 percentage points more than do private workers at corresponding educational levels. But people other than teachers who work for state and local governments vote at a prodigiously higher rate. State employees are 12 percent more likely to vote, and local employees are 16 percent more likely to go to the polls. This effect is particularly strong among the least educated, although the impact of working for the government does not diminish with education nearly as sharply as was the case with our 1972 analysis.

Although only a minority of state and local jobs are filled by patronage, these positions encompass whatever patronage there is. Thus the difference shown in table 5.2 between federal workers and teachers, on the one hand, and other government employees on the other, display the impact of patronage on turnout. Unfortunately, our inability to identify each individual state prevents us both from isolating those public employees who live in patronage states and from examining the effects of concurrent elections in 1974.

Table 5.2.   **Turnout of Government Employees by Education and Level of Government, in 1974 (in Percent)**

	Increase in turnout over private employees		
Years of education	*Teachers and federal employees*	*State employees*	*Local employees*
0–8 (grammar school)	5	14	18
9–12 (high school)	5	13	17
1–3 college	4	12	16
4 college	5	12	16
5+ college	4	10	11
Total	5	13	17

Note: The entry in each cell is the probit estimate (see appendix C) of the increase in percentage turnout over a private employee with the same education. For example, local government employees who had not gone beyond the eighth grade had a turnout rate 18 percentage points higher than other members of the labor force with this amount of schooling.

6: SOME IMPLICATIONS

Our main task in this chapter will be to explore the political implications of variations in turnout by comparing voters to the entire adult population. Before doing this, let us summarize our conclusions.

The core finding is the transcendent importance of education. From this we have developed our fundamental proposition: the personal qualities that raise the probability of voting are the skills that make learning about politics easier and more gratifying and reduce the difficulties of voting. Education increases one's capacity for understanding complex and intangible subjects such as politics, as well as encouraging the ethic of civic responsibility. Moreover, schools provide experience with a variety of bureaucratic problems, such as coping with requirements, filling out forms, and meeting deadlines.

The second most important variable is age, which we consider a measure of individual experience. Successive exposure to elections and to the bureaucratic hurdles of life in a complex society imparts skills that many young people lack when they reach the age of voter eligibility. This is particularly true of the uneducated, which strengthens our belief that life experience is a substitute for education. The positive relationship between age and turnout continues for much more of the life cycle than observers have thought. Once other demographic characteristics have been controlled, voting rates continue to rise well into the seventies. Theories that physical infirmities or "disengagement" from broader concerns cause a decline in voting are not supported by our data. We could also find little evidence for the notion that young people begin to vote more as they assume adult roles. Students vote more than their nonstudent counterparts, and while marriage (an adult role) does increase turnout, this effect is found among all age groups and is rather slight among young people.

Being a college student and having a spouse affect turnout, but we found little evidence that other types of social environment do so. The interpersonal surroundings associated with higher status occupations do not seem to generate higher voting rates. And if we think that high incomes and prestigious jobs determine one's friends and neighbors, we find no indication that this sort of environment has any appreciable effect on voting because there is no relationship between turnout and high income or occupations. A rich person is no more likely to vote than someone with an average income; the same is true for those with elevated as opposed to middle-level jobs.

The lack of relationship between top incomes and occupations and voting leads us also to reject the proposition that voting is motivated by a larger number of material possessions, usually called a "stake in the system." We did find high turnout by people with a stake in another sort of system—the patronage system that affects their jobs.

Propositions about the effect on electoral participation of various subnational "political cultures" had a mixed fate. Taking everything else into account, people who live in the South do vote appreciably less than other Americans. No other distinctions of this sort were related to turnout by the general public, however. People living in states that are particularly hospitable to civic uplift are not more likely to vote than residents of states less touched by the spirit of reform.

Free time is not a resource that is important for voting. No category of people that we could identify as having more free time voted more. Whatever differences we could find in this respect were in the opposite direction: the unemployed vote less; occupational groups with more free time vote less. People in certain life circumstances are presumably more likely to be distracted from voting by other concerns, whether they are looking for a spouse, for a job, or for a suitable lifetime career. The depressing effect of any of these experiences (to the extent that we can make valid inferences from our data) is slight, however.

Why does it matter that so many Americans fail to vote? Low turnout strikes many observers as evidence of widespread disaffection and thus seems to be an indictment of a political system that fails to inspire this elementary act of participation. Doubtless this interpretation will persist, despite accumulating evidence that people who express alienated opinions are no less likely to vote (Citrin 1978). One can also find arguments that the country is better off without the votes of its least interested and least informed citizens. People who consider voting more trouble than it is worth are likely (so this line of argument goes) to make the wrong sorts of choices, should they ever find themselves in a voting booth. Irrespective of the merits of either viewpoint, it is possible that low turnout does contribute to a diminished sense of the government's legitimacy: officials elected by such a small proportion of the population may be considered worthy of less support than those chosen in an election in which almost everyone took part.

Another line of inquiry is concerned not with the relative size of the voting population but with the differences between it and all Americans. Because everyone does not have the same likelihood of voting, voters as a whole differ from the entire population of adult citizens. The size and character of these differences define the extent to which voters are "descriptively representative" (Pitkin 1967, chapter 4) of the population and permit a step (the only one we will take) on the road to understanding the political implications of variations in turnout. We will compare voters to all citizens with respect to both demographic characteristics and various measures of political inclination—party identification and attitudes on issues. This exercise is similar to our comparison in chapter 4 of actual 1972 voters with the larger hypothetical voting population that would result from liberalized election laws. Then we were talking about an increase of 9 percentage points; excluded from the comparison were many millions of nonvoters. That exercise did not yield very impressive differences. Here we expect to find bigger gaps, since the two groups being compared are of such different size.

The technique is the same as in chapter 4: we compare the proportion of voters with that of the entire sample comprised of members of various demographic groups. For example, the college educated account for 26 percent of the total adult population and 32.3 percent of voters (columns 1 and 2 in table 6.1). Subtracting the first figure from the second reveals the extent to which Americans who have been to college comprise a larger share (6.3 percent greater) of voters than of the population. The percentage difference is less than zero for groups that comprise a smaller share of voters than of all citizens, such as people who have not completed the eighth grade (see column 3 of table 6.1).

As table 6.1 shows, voters differ substantially from all citizens on a number of demographic dimensions. Starting with education, we find that people without a high school diploma comprise 36.4 percent of the population but only 29 percent of voters, a difference of −7.4 percent. Those with family incomes below $10,000 are 55.2 percent of the population and just 48 percent of all voters, a difference of −7.2 percent. The young, the unmarried, Southerners, the unemployed, minorities, and people who moved within two years of the 1974 election all comprise a smaller share of voters than of the population as a whole. Women and students are about the same proportion. People who are white, well educated, well-to-do, middle-aged, married, Northerners, government employees, and residentially stable account for a proportion of voters larger than their share of the population.

These percentage differences reflect each group's size as well as its turnout rate. Although Puerto Ricans are light voters, their percentage difference does not appear substantial—a mere .3 percent—because they are not a very big part of the total population. Another way to view the problem, without considering group size, is to ascertain the extent to which each group's electoral strength is inflated or deflated by its voting rate. We measure this by the simple ratio of a group's share of the voters to its

Table 6.1. Demographic Comparison of Voters with the Adult Population in 1972

	(1) Percent of the adult citizen population [a]		(2) Percent of voters [b]		(3) (2)−(1)		(4) (2)÷(1)	
Years of education								
0–4	3.6		2.0		−1.6		.56	
5–7	6.4		4.7		−1.7		.73	
8	10.0	36.4	8.8	29.0	−1.2	−7.4	.88	.80
9–11	16.4		13.5		−2.9		.82	
12	37.6		38.7		1.1		1.03	
1–3 college	14.2		16.8		2.6		1.18	
4 college	7.3	26.0	9.4	32.3	2.1	6.3	1.29	1.24
5+ college	4.5		6.1		1.6		1.36	
Family income								
Under $2,000	6.2		4.3		−1.9		.69	
$2,000–$7,499	34.0	55.2	29.0	48.0	−5.0	−7.2	.85	.87
$7,500–$9,999	15.0		14.7		−0.3		.98	
$10,000–$14,999	25.6		28.1		2.5		1.10	
$15,000–$24,999	14.5	19.3	17.6	23.8	3.1	4.5	1.21	1.23
$25,000 and over	4.8		6.2		1.4		1.29	
Age								
18–24	17.9	32.5	14.2	27.9	−3.7	−4.6	.79	.86
25–31	14.6		13.7		−0.9		.94	
32–36	8.2		8.3		0.1		1.01	
37–69	49.7		54.8		5.1		1.10	
70–78	6.5		6.6		0.1		1.02	
79 and over	3.1		2.4		−0.7		.77	

Women	53.2	52.7	−0.5	.99
Unmarried or separated	30.2	26.4	−3.8	.87
Students, age 18–24	2.7	2.8	−0.1	1.04
Southerners	25.6	21.6	−4.0	.84
Government employees	10.2	12.6	2.4	1.24
Unemployed	2.7	2.2	−0.5	.81
Blacks	9.8	8.2	−1.6	.84
Puerto Ricans[c]	.6	.3	−1.6	.84
Chicanos[c]	1.9	1.3	−0.6	.68
Length of residence[c]	33.4	20.8	−12.6	.62
less than 4 months	7.3	3.1	−3.6	.42
4–6 months	5.7	3.0	−2.7	.53
7–11 months	4.5	2.6	−1.9	.58
1–2 years	15.9	12.1	−3.8	.76
3–5 years	16.1	16.3	0.2	1.01
6–9 years	13.5	15.8	2.3	1.17
10 or more years	37.1	46.6	9.5	1.26

[a] Citizens over the age of seventeen for whom turnout was reported.
[b] Voters in the general election.
[c] Estimated using 1974 data.

share of the citizen population (column 4 in table 6.1). Ratios smaller than 1.0 indicate underrepresentation, while ratios over 1.0 show overrepresentation. Measured this way, Puerto Ricans are severely underrepresented; their share of all voters is just half (.50) of their share of the potential electorate.

As we see in table 6.1, a number of groups are significantly underrepresented at the polls, while others are substantially overrepresented. The least educated, the very poor, Puerto Ricans, Chicanos, and people who moved in the year before the 1974 election are all underrepresented by between one-third and one-half. In addition, people without a high school diploma or below the median income, those who live in the South, the young, the elderly, the unemployed, the unmarried, and blacks show voting strength reduced by a least 15 percent. On the other hand, college graduates are overrepresented by nearly one-third, as are people who earn more than $25,000. Government employees' strength at the polls is 24 percent greater than their share of the population.

In short, voters are not a microcosm of the entire body of citizens but a distorted sample that exaggerates the size of some groups and minimizes that of others. Some categories of Americans exert only half the voting strength that they would have if everyone had an equal probability of voting, while the electoral power of other groups is inflated by more than 25 percent. The most underrepresented Americans include those who are disadvantaged in other ways as well: the poor, the uneducated, and racial minorities. (Also underrepresented are people whom it is difficult to consider disadvantaged, such as youth and people who are not married or have moved shortly before the election.)

Some writers claim that because turnout among the disadvantaged is low, politicians do not consider it necessary to enact social welfare policies that would be in their interests (Reiter 1979). This assertion assumes that the poor have views about issues and parties that differ markedly from other people's and thus that if turnout variations disappeared, voters would have different and presumably more liberal views than they do at present. The initial assumption—that preferences for parties and policies vary greatly from one social class to the next—is not strongly supported in the literature (Dawson, 1973). In any event, we can test the basic proposition about the political implications of variations in turnout by seeing whether the substantial demographic differences displayed in table 6.1 will be paralleled by comparable disparities in the political orientations of voters and all voting-age citizens. For this purpose we must shift from the census data to the 1972 National Election Study of the University of Michigan Center for Political Studies.

In table 6.2 we compare the party identification of voters and of all Americans to see to what extent turnout rates distort the electoral expression of party preferences. The proportion of Democrats is identical in the two groups—51.4 percent of all citizens and 51.3 percent of voters identify with the Democratic party. Republicans, on the other hand, are slightly overrepresented; they comprise 36.0 percent of the total population and 39.7 percent of voters. Independents are substantially underrepresented; their low voting rate reduces their electoral strength by about one-quarter. The political consequence of this pattern is a Republican gain of nearly 4 percentage points, a genuine advantage, although fairly small compared to the demographic disparities displayed in table 6.1.[1]

All other political differences between voters and the general population are considerably smaller than this gap of 3.7 percentage points. Moreover, these other differences, slight as they are, do not have a consistent bias for any particular political orientation, as table 6.3 shows. On some issues voters are a shade more liberal than the entire population; and on others they are a trifle more conservative. And sometimes both liberal and conservative viewpoints are overrepresented among voters, while those who give "undecided" or "moderate" responses are underrepresented. In short, on these issues voters are virtually a carbon copy of the citizen population. Those most likely to be underrepresented are people who lack opinions.

Contrary to the conservative bias alleged by some scholars

Table 6.2. Partisan Composition of Voters and the Adult Population in 1972

	(1) Percent of the adult citizen population[a]		(2) Percent of voters[b]		(3) (2)−(1)		(4) (2)÷(1)	
Strong Democrat	14.5%		15.7%		1.2		1.08	
Weak Democrat	26.1	51.4	25.1	51.3	−1.0	−0.1	.96	1.00
Independent Democrat	10.8		10.5		−0.3		.97	
Independent	12.5		9.1		−3.4		.73	
Independent Republican	10.9		11.3		0.4		1.04	
Weak Republican	14.2	36.0	15.4	39.7	1.2	3.7	1.08	1.10
Strong Republican	10.9		13.0		2.1		1.19	
Total	99.9%		100.1%		—		—	
(N)	(2,246)		(1,651)		—		—	

Source: Authors' analysis of data from Center for Political Studies 1972 National Election Study. The total number of voters in this table (1,651) is less than the number of voters in table 4.4. In this table the total number is the number of people who reported that they voted; in table 4.4 it is the predicted number of voters based on equation 2.

[a] Citizens over the age of seventeen for whom turnout was reported.
[b] Voters in the 1972 general election.

(Amundsen 1977, pp. 136–37), voters are not disproportionately hostile to social welfare policies. People holding the view that "the government should just let each person get ahead on his own" are very slightly underrepresented among voters, but so are people who believe that "the government should see to it that every person has a job and a good standard of living." The people who are overrepresented on this issue are those who take a middle-of-the-road position. There is a conservative bias on the question of federal medical insurance, but it amounts to a difference of just over 1 percentage point.

On other sorts of issues the differences are also small and more consistently in the direction of liberal, not conservative, overrepresentation. Advocates of busing comprise .3 percent more of voters than of the general population. People favoring the right of women to have abortions are 44.6 percent of voters and 42.6 percent of all citizens. The findings are similar for legalizing marijuana and women's equality. Finally, both self-described liberals *and* conservatives are slightly overrepresented at the polls, at the expense of moderates and people who say they have no ideological tendency.

All the differences in table 6.3 are small and statistically insignificant. The tiny gaps (which may well not be real) suggest that on these political questions people who vote are representative of the population as a whole. The demographic disparities we reported earlier have fewer consequences than those bare figures alone suggested. Given current political alignments, these demographic biases do not translate into discernible overrepresentation of particular policy constituencies. As long as attitudes on issues are so weakly related to social class and race, the poor and minorities will find enough allies to avoid political weakness in proportion to their own voting rates.

There may be other issues on which the preferences of voters differ significantly from those of the entire population. There may also be issues that are salient only to particular subgroups. Citizens who are underrepresented at the polls on these issues, other things being equal, are less able to command the attention of elected officials and affect their decisions on public policy.

Table 6.3. Attitudes of Voters and the Adult Population in 1972

	(1) Percent of the adult citizen population[a]	(2) Percent of voters[b]	(3) (2)−(1)	(4) (2)÷(1)
Government should see that everyone has a job and a good standard of living	31.4	30.6	−0.8	.97
Middle of the road	23.4	25.4	2.0	1.09
People should get ahead on their own	45.2	44.0	−1.2	.97
Government should provide a health insurance plan	44.9	43.8	−1.1	.98
Middle of the road	14.6	14.2	−0.4	.97
Medical expenses should be paid by individuals and through private insurance	40.6	42.0	1.4	1.03
Bus to achieve integration	8.8	9.1	0.3	1.03
Middle of the road	4.8	5.5	0.7	1.15
Keep children in neighborhood schools	86.4	85.4	−1.0	.99
Legalize marijuana	22.2	24.1	1.9	1.09
Middle of the road	10.8	11.4	0.6	1.06
Increase penalties for use	67.0	64.5	−2.5	.96

Category	(a)	(b)	Difference	Ratio
Abortion should never be forbidden	24.9	26.2	1.3	1.06
Abortion should be permitted if the woman would have difficulty caring for the child	17.7	18.4	0.7	1.04
combined	42.6	44.6	2.0	1.05
Abortion should be permitted only if the life and health of the woman is in danger	46.8	45.8	−1.0	.98
Abortion should never be permitted	10.6	9.6	−1.0	.91
combined	57.4	55.4	−2.0	.97
Women deserve equal role in business and government	49.1	51.0	1.9	1.04
Middle of the road	20.0	21.2	1.2	1.06
Women's place is in the home	30.9	27.8	−3.1	.90
Self-described liberals	25.9	26.6	0.7	1.03
Moderates	37.4	35.4	−2.0	.95
Conservatives	36.7	38.0	1.3	1.04

Source: Authors' analysis of data from Center for Political Studies 1972 National Election Study.

[a] Citizens over the age of seventeen for whom turnout was reported.
[b] Voters in the '1972 general election.

If future political cleavages more closely parallel education, income, race, and age differences, then the consequences of variations in turnout will be felt in the fate of policy proposals. For the present, it appears that advocates of both sides of major controversial policy issues are represented among voters in proportion to their numbers in the general population.

APPENDIX A: SAMPLES FOR THE STUDY OF TURNOUT

Estimates of turnout in sample surveys are always somewhat higher than those based on the total number of ballots cast by the aggregate voting-age population. Since 1948, reported turnout in sample surveys has ranged between 5 percent and 17 percent higher than the aggregate estimates. (For extended discussions of this problem see Campbell et al. 1960, pp. 94–96; Roper 1961; Andrews 1966; Clausen 1969; U.S. Bureau of the Census 1972, pp. 7–8.) The 1972 election is no exception, as table A demonstrates. The commonly cited aggregate turnout figure is 55.5 percent, while reported turnout from our Current Population Survey sample is 66.7 percent, a gap of 11.2 percent. The turnout reported by the Michigan study is 72.8 percent, 17.3 percent above the aggregate estimate.

Observers of this persistent gap between survey reports and the "real" figure sometimes jump to the conclusion that the discrepancy reflects only misreporting by respondents reluctant to admit they did not do their civic duty. This is just one of a number of contributing factors, however. First, it should be understood that the aggregate percentage *underestimates* turnout. The denominator of the percentage is an estimate of the total number of people of voting age (U.S. Bureau of the Census 1972, pp. 1, 3). This includes millions of people who are ineligible to vote: aliens, inmates of prisons and mental institutions, and ex-convicts, who cannot vote in many states (Andrews 1966, pp. 642–44; Zitter and Starsinic 1966; Clausen 1969, pp. 589–91; U.S. Bureau of the Census 1972, p. 3). If noncitizens are removed from the denominator of the aggregate computation, the

Table A. Estimates of Voter Turnout in the 1972 and 1974 General Elections

Estimate (in percent)	*1972*	*1974*
Voting-age population casting votes for president/House of Representatives [a]	55.5	36.1
Citizens of voting age casting votes for president/House of Representatives [b]	56.7	37.2
Estimated turnout from Current Population Survey [c]	66.7	48.7
Estimated turnout from Center for Political Studies, National Election Study [d]	72.8	53.7

[a] *Statistical Abstract of the United States, 1977*, p. 508.

[b] For 1972, letter to the authors from Gilbert R. Felton, Bureau of the Census, Population Division, December 29, 1976. For 1974, we used the estimate from U.S. Bureau of the Census (1976) that 2.8 percent of the voting-age population were noncitizens. We deleted this proportion from the total voting-age population and recomputed the percentage who voted.

[c] Our analysis of the Current Population Survey data. We excluded from the sample all noncitizens and cases where the respondent did not know if a vote had been cast. This produced a weighted N of 128,582 in 1972 and 129,801 in 1974.

[d] In 1972 this was variable 0477 ($N = 2,283$); in 1974 it was variable 2319 (weighted $N = 2,512$).

turnout estimate rises from 55.5 percent to 56.7 percent. The numerator of the aggregate percentage represents the total number of valid counted votes cast for president. This excludes people who cast a spoiled ballot (they think they voted, but their vote is not counted), those who go to the polls but do not vote for president, and people whose votes for miscellaneous write-in candidates are not tallied. The best available estimates indicate that 2 to 3 million people are "uncounted voters." (Campbell et al. 1960, pp. 94–95; Bureau of the Census 1971, p. 8.)

Survey estimates, on the other hand, overestimate turnout. Most surveys do not include some categories of people who are eligible to vote but are rather unlikely to do so. Students in dormitories, people living on military reservations in the United States, and inmates of institutions for the elderly are all left out of the census sample. The institutional population amounted to 5.8

million people in 1970. In addition to such deliberate exclusions, surveys consistently tend to undersample some demographic groups with low turnout rates and to oversample others that are more likely to vote. The census sample includes the "rooming house population," a low-turnout group excluded from the Michigan sample (Campbell et al. 1960, pp. 94–95; Clausen 1969, pp. 592–96; U.S. Bureau of the Census 1972, pp. 8, 13; Traugott and Katosh 1979).

The 6.1 percent discrepancy in reported turnout between the census and Michigan studies can be attributed to two other factors. First, the Census Bureau had a much higher interview completion rate. In 1972 it completed interviews with 94 percent of those selected for its sample, as compared with 84 percent for the postelection interview in the Michigan study. (Center for Political Studies 1973, p. xiii; U.S. Bureau of the Census 1976a, p. 89.) Respondents whose postelection interviews could not be completed tended to come from groups with lower turnout rates. (Campbell et al. 1960, p. 95; Clausen 1969, pp. 592–95.) Second, the Census Bureau asked only a few political questions in its November interviews; the political content of the Michigan preelection and postelection interviews in 1972 was heavy. Furthermore, most of the respondents to the 1974 Michigan survey had also been interviewed in 1972. The evidence is strong that these repeated political stimulations caused some Michigan respondents to vote (Yalch 1976; Traugott and Katosh 1979). Needless to say, these points suggest further advantages of the census survey for the study of turnout.

So far, we have explored reasons why people who are interviewed might vote more heavily than the population as a whole does. We have yet to consider the problem of respondents who do not vote but who tell an interviewer that they have done so. The extent of this misreporting can be established precisely for some Michigan samples because the researchers checked their respondents' claims against the official voting records. Of the 1964 respondents, 8 percent falsely claimed to have voted, as did 11 percent of the 1976 sample (Clausen 1969, pp. 596–98, 601; Traugott and Katosh 1979).

The census data probably include a roughly comparable amount of overreporting, although we cannot say just how much. The most recent Michigan "vote validation" study (Traugott and Katosh 1979; Weisberg 1979) provides assurance that this problem has not distorted our findings. *Misreporting is not strongly related to demographic characteristics*, although it is a bit more common among the very young and the very poor. Nineteen percent of those with incomes under $6,000 and 18 percent of people aged eighteen to twenty-four falsely claimed that they voted in 1976. Even with the benefit of this exaggeration, these groups still report low turnout. In other words, correcting for misreporting strengthens the existing relationships between turnout and age or income. The only exception to this comforting conclusion is blacks, who are twice as likely as whites to say that they voted when they did not. This fact should be remembered when assessing the finding (mentioned above in chapter 5) that blacks vote at a slightly higher rate than whites when other variables are controlled.

DESCRIPTION OF THE VARIABLES
AND CODING PROCEDURES

Individual Level Data

All individual level data were taken from the November 1972 and November 1974 Bureau of the Census Current Population Surveys described above.

Turnout: Did not vote = 0; voted = 1.

Race: Whites and other races = 0; blacks = 1.

Education: 0–4 years = 1; 5–7 years = 2; 8 years = 3; 9–11 years = 4; 12 years = 5; 1–3 years of college = 6; 4 years of college = 7; 5+ years of college = 8.

Income: Under $1,000 = 1; $1,000–$1,999 = 2; $2,000–$2,999 = 3; $3,000–$3,999 = 4; $4,000–$4,999 = 5; $5,000–$5,999 = 6; $6,000–$7,499 = 7; $7,500–$9,999 = 8; $10,000–$14,999 = 9; $15,000–$24,999 = 10; $25,000 and over = 11.

Age: The number coded was the actual age of the respondent. (People over the age of 99 were coded "99" by the Bureau of the Census.)

Occupation: Each of the following occupational groups was represented by a dummy variable: professional and technical; managers and administrators; farmers; sales and clerical workers; nondomestic service workers; and farm laborers.

Sex: Male = 0; female = 1.

Marital Status: Two dummy variables were used to estimate the three categories: Unmarried but living with relatives = 1; other = 0; unmarried and not living with relatives = 1; other = 0.

Students: Students = 1; others = 0.

Unable to Work: Unable to work = 1; others = 0.

Government Employees: Government employees = 1; others = 0. In 1974 each of the following groups of government employees was represented by a separate dummy variable: federal employees and teachers, state government employees, local government employees. Initially, postal workers, other federal employees, and teachers were treated as separate variables, but preliminary analysis indicated that these categories could be combined into a single variable.

Chicanos: Chicano = 1; others = 0.

Puerto Ricans: Puerto Rican = 1; others = 0.

Unemployed: Employed = 0; unemployed = 1.

Weeks Unemployed: The actual number of consecutive weeks unemployed, coded 0 through 99.

Length of Residence at Current Address: Less than 1 month = .083; 1–3 months = .167; 4–6 months = .417; 7–11 months = .75; 1–2 years = 1.5; 3–5 years = 4.0; 6–9 years = 7.5; 10 years or more = 10.0.

Lives in Trailer: lives in house, apartment, flat, rooming house, hotel = 0; lives in mobile home or trailer = 1.

Contextual Variables

Region: North = 0; South = 1 (Alabama, Arkansas, Florida, Georgia, Louisiana, Mississippi, North Carolina, South Carolina, Tennessee, Texas, and Virginia).

Rural Nonfarm: Rural nonfarm residents = 1; other = 0.

Patronage States: Patronage states = 1 (Indiana, Massachusetts, Illinois, Maryland, New York, Missouri, New Jersey, Pennsylvania, Rhode Island, and West Virginia); others = 0.

Reform States: Reform states = 1 (California, Wisconsin, Minnesota, Oregon, South Dakota, Washington, Nebraska, Utah, Idaho, and North Dakota); others = 0.

Gubernatorial Election: Concurrent gubernatorial election = 1; no gubernatorial election = 0.

APPENDIX C:
PROBIT ESTIMATES

In the probit model the conditional probability of voting $p(x)$ is defined as

$$p(x) = F(\beta_0 + \beta_1 + \ldots + \beta_n X_n)$$

or, equivalently,

$$F^{-1}(p(x)) = \beta_0 + \beta_1 X_1 + \ldots + \beta_n X_n,$$

where $F(\ )$ represents the value of the cumulative standard normal distribution. Using numerical maximum methods (because the normal equations are nonlinear in the parameters), the parameters $B_0, B_1 \ldots, B_n$ can be estimated.

Figure A illustrates the differences between the OLS model and the probit model. The OLS model assumes a linear relationship between the parameters and the probability of voting; a unit increase in an independent variable has the same impact on the probability of voting, regardless of the values of the other independent variables. For example, consider an OLS equation in which an individual characteristic (represented by a dummy variable) has a coefficient of $-.13$. We would conclude that this characteristic decreases the probability of voting by 13 percent ($-.13 \times 1 \times 100\%$). That is, a person who is otherwise 90 percent likely to vote would have a probability of voting of 77 percent as a result of this being scored a "one" on this variable. The effect would be the same for everyone: a probability of voting of 60 percent would be reduced to 47 percent; a 40 percent probability would now be 27 percent; and a person who is otherwise 10 percent likely to vote would have a probability of voting of $-.03$!

As suggested by this example and by figure A, with an OLS equation the predicted probability of voting will not necessarily be confined to the 0–1 interval. That is, with OLS some values of the independent variables may yield estimated probabilities that are less than 0 or greater than 1. The probit estimates are always between 0 and 1.

There are ways to compensate for the linearity of the co-efficients in the OLS model. The most common approach is the inclusion of interaction terms that allow the effect of one independent variable to vary with the value of another independent variable. A final problem still remains, however. With OLS the error variance is not constant across all observations. The variance of the residuals will be small for predicted probabilities close to either 0 or 1, while the variance will be much larger for predictions between .4 and .6. As a result, the OLS estimates are inefficient.

A probit estimate is not as easy to interpret as the familiar OLS estimate. Unlike OLS, the probit coefficient does not directly represent an estimate of the amount of change in the dependent variable that results from a unit increase in the independent variable. Rather, with probit analysis, the coefficient is an estimate of the amount of change on the cumulative standard normal dis-

Figure A. Comparison of Ordinary Least Squares (OLS)
Model with Probit Model

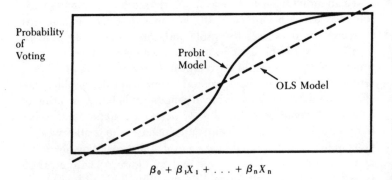

tribution that would result from a change in one unit in the independent variable, with the other variables held constant.

To estimate the aggregate marginal effect of a single variable on the *probability* of a particular subpopulation voting, the following procedure was followed. (1) For each respondent in the subsample, the probit equation (see equation 1) was used to compute a probit estimate, which was then converted to a probability by evaluating that number on the cumulative standard normal distribution. (2) To estimate the marginal impact of education, for example, the same procedure was followed, except that for each respondent the value of the lowest educational category was substituted in place of his actual education. (3) For each respondent these two probabilities were subtracted. In this example, the difference between the two probabilities is the effect of the individual's level of education, compared to being in the lowest educational category, on the probability of voting. (4) The final step is to aggregate these individual probabilities across people in the subpopulation. To do this the sample was reweighted so that it was representative of the civilian, citizen voting-age population, excluding the District of Columbia. This reweighting was accomplished by multiplying, for each case, the original sample weight by ten (the inverse of the subsampling proportion). This yields a reweighted N of 121,758. This number is slightly less than the weighted N reported earlier, mainly because respondents who had missing data on the income variable or were from the District of Columbia were deleted from the probit analysis and, secondarily, because of the random selection of cases in the subsampling procedure. The weighted mean of the individual differences in the two probabilities is the estimated aggregate effect of the variable, in this example, education. This weighted mean can be computed for specific subpopulations such as income groups. In this way we can estimate the marginal effect of education on the probability of voting for each income group (see table 2.4). See Theil (1971, pp. 628–31); Finney (1971); Goldberger (1964, pp. 248–51); Cox (1970, pp. 1–29); Pindyck and Rubinfeld (1976, pp. 227–47); Aldrich and Cnudde (1975, pp. 571–608); Hanushek and Jackson (1977, chapter 7).

Equation 1. Estimates of the Effect of Demographic Variables on Turnout in 1972

Variable	Probit estimate	Standard error
(Constant)	−2.0050	.1311
Education squared	.0250	.0015
Income	.0567	.0072
Occupation		
Professional and technical	.2186	.0726
Managers and administrators	.0936	.0700
Farmers	.5407	.1366
Sales and clerical	.3611	.0477
Nondomestic service workers	.1636	.0641
Farm laborers	−.1630	.1721
Blacks	.1123	.0526
Age	.0505	.0052
Age squared	−.00027	.00006
Age for Southerners	−.0034	.0008
Age squared for women	−.000019	.000012
Unmarried and living with relatives × age squared	−.000126	.000016
Not living with relatives × age	−.01247	.00387
Not living with relatives × age squared	.000119	.000058
Student	.5419	.0969
Unable to work	−.6445	.1102
Rural nonfarm	−.0739	.0369
Government employee	.1389	.0662
Government employee with no college in a patronage state	.3922	.1422
Gubernatorial election in a patronage state	.1878	.0496
Evening and/or Saturday registration hours	.1771	.0333
Irregular weekday registration hours	−.1125	.0517
Closing date for voter registration	−.0073	.0019

Number of cases = 8,334
Percentage of cases correctly predicted = 72.9
−2 times the log likelihood ratio = 1560.1
Degrees of freedom = 25

APPENDIX D: DATA ON STATE VOTER
REGISTRATION PROVISIONS

Obtaining information about each state's voting laws was more difficult than we had expected. Several publications contain lists of state registration laws for the 1972 general election (League of Women Voters Education Fund 1972; Library of Congress 1972; Reitman and Davidson 1972; Thornton 1972; U.S. Senate 1972). Unfortunately, none of these compilations reflects *Dunn* v. *Blumstein* and the numerous state-level responses to this decision that changed residency requirements or closing dates for the November election.

We tried to obtain this information by sending a one-page questionnaire to each state's chief election official. They were quick to respond to our inquiry; forty-one individuals replied within a few weeks, although not always with accurate responses. A check with the statutes themselves indicated that more than a third of the returned questionnaires had at least one error. We think that this reflects the passage of time since the 1972 election, changes both in personnel and in state laws, and possible confusion of presidential and other elections with respect to laws.

We finally gathered these data directly from the Library of the Boalt School of Law on the Berkeley Campus of the University of California. The material for each state includes not only the state code but all relevant state and federal court decisions and also state attorney general opinions, if federal legislation or court decisions altered the application of state statutes.

In coding these data it was necessary to reconcile the complexities of real life with the more simplistic world of quantitative analysis. One set of problems of this sort was presented by states that mandated different procedures for different areas, usually on the basis of population. For example, Iowa, Minnesota, Missouri, Ohio, and Wisconsin exempted their less populous counties from registration requirements. Since in each case only a small fraction of the state population was excluded and we could not identify our respondents' counties, we ignored this deviation from the laws governing most of the states' residents.

A second set of problems was encountered with the differences between state laws that required a particular practice, allowed it, or forbade it. We have no way of knowing the extent to which permissive state legislation is actually exploited at the local level. For example, many states authorize the appointment of deputy registrars. This is not the same thing as requiring the deputizing of a fixed number of registrars to go from door to door or sit at tables in shopping centers and student unions. Lacking knowledge of the extent to which registrars are appointed (not to mention the vigor with which they do their work), we could only distinguish between states that permit deputy registrars and those that do not. On the question of regular hours for registration offices, we classified as "irregular" all states that prescribed any schedule less than regular business hours five days a week. We combined states that required such schedules with those that did not legislate on the issue when our preliminary analysis showed no differences in turnout. States that required evening and/or Saturday office hours were separated from those that did not. (A token Saturday or two was not enough.)

In short, many matters are often left to local officials and the initiative of local interest groups and parties. In view of these large areas of discretion, we acknowledge that our data do not necessarily describe the reality of administration and enforcement at the local level. They do describe state-level enactments, which still vary considerably.

We coded the legal provisions in the following way:

Residency Requirement: The coding was done so that the variable is the *de facto* residency requirement in the state. In other words, if a state has no residency requirement but the last day new residents can register is thirty days before the election, then the state has a thirty-day *de facto* residency requirement. Even though there is no explicit residency requirement, new residents must have been in the state at least thirty days prior to the election in order to register. This state was coded as having a thirty-day *de facto* residency requirement, not a zero-day requirement. Similarly, a state that had a closing date of thirty days but a special provision enabling new residents to register until seven days before the election was coded as having a seven-day *de facto* residency requirement.

Closing Date: The number coded was the number of days before the election when a resident could last register to vote.

Where to Register: County office only = 1; other = 0. Precinct or neighborhood locations below the town level = 1; other = 0.

Deputy Registrars: Allowed = 0; not allowed = 1.

Monday through Friday Registration Office Hours: Regular hours (forty hours a week, every week) = 0; irregular hours = 1.

Evening and/or Saturday Registration Hours: Not required = 0; regularly required = 1.

Absentee Registration by Mail: Permitted for ill, disabled, and/or absent from voting unit = 0; none permitted = 1. Universal absentee registration = 1; other = 0.

Years before Purging: The number of years of nonvoting after which one's name is removed from the registration rolls. Number of years coded = 2–8; no purging = 8. (Our preliminary estimates were made using two variables. The first was coded 2–8 years, with no purging coded 0. A separate dummy variable was included (1 = no purging) to estimate this category. There is no significant loss of information by using the single variable described above.

Hours Polls Open: The number coded was the number of hours the polls are open on election day.

Appendix E

Preliminary Probit Estimates of the Effect of Demographic Variables and Registration Laws on Turnout in 1972

Variable	Probit estimate	Standard error
(Constant)	−2.7646	.2740
Education	.1838	.0451
Education squared	.0121	.0050
Age	.0706	.0045
Age Squared	−.0006	.0001
Race	−.0189	.0549
Region	−.1279	.0546
Residency requirement	.0025	.0018
Closing date	−.0089	.0021
No deputy registrars	.0161	.0448
Irregular office hours	−.1540	.0547
Open evening and/or Saturday	.01271	.0398
Years before purging	.0098	.0105
Register only at county seat	−.0165	.0494
Register in neighborhood	.0564	.0484
No absentee registration	−.1054	.0421
Universal absentee registration	−.0891	.0627
Hours polls open	.0357	.0175
Gubernatorial election	.0441	.0369
No senatorial election	−.0293	.0385

Number of cases = 7,936
−2 times the log likelihood ratio = 1160.27
Degrees of freedom = 19

Appendix F

Equation 2.   Final Estimates of the Effect of Demographic Variables and Registration Laws on Turnout in 1972

Variable	Probit estimate	Standard error
(Constant)	−2.7001	.2410
Education	.1847	.0120
Education squared	.0120	.0050
Age	.0707	.0045
Age squared	−.0006	.0001
Region	−.1371	.0413
Closing date	−.0073	.0015
Irregular office hours	−.1005	.0438
Open evening and/or Saturday	.1253	.0345
No absentee registration	−.0909	.0403
Hours polls open	.0336	.0159
Gubernatorial election	.0634	.0338

Number of cases = 7,936
Percentage of cases correctly predicted = 71.4
−2 times the log likelihood ratio = 1154.66
Degrees of freedom = 11

Note: Estimates for the variables deleted from this equation are given in appendix E.

Appendix G

The Effect of Registration Requirements on the Likelihood That an Individual Would Vote in the 1972 Election (in Percent)

Probability of an individual's voting (%)	30-day closing date	Irregular office hours	No Saturday or evening registration	No absentee registration
20	−6.7	−2.9	−3.8	−2.6
30	−8.1	−3.6	−4.7	−3.2
40	−8.7	−3.9	−5.1	−3.5
50	−8.7	−4.0	−5.5	−3.6
60	−8.2	−3.8	−4.9	−3.4
70	−8.1	−3.4	−3.4	−3.1
80	−5.6	−2.9	−3.4	−2.4
90	−3.3	−1.7	−2.1	−1.5

Note: The effect on turnout of a registration provision depends on the probability that an individual would otherwise vote. The cell entry is the estimated effect of the provision on an individual with the specified probability of voting. For example, a person who was otherwise 40 percent likely to vote was 8.7 percent less likely to do so if he lived in a state with a thirty-day closing date. A person who was 90 percent likely to vote was only 3.3 percent less likely to do so as a result of a thirty-day closing date. These estimates were derived by using the cumulative normal distribution to evaluate the probit estimates in equation 2 in appendix F.

NOTES

Chapter 1

1. Many political commentators say that low turnout reflects popular dissatisfaction with the available choices; if only the right candidates or parties came along, Americans would flock to the polls. All the evidence shows, however, that abstention from voting has little to do with popular evaluations of the candidates. People who find both presidential candidates equally attractive or unappealing are as likely to vote as those who have strong preferences (Brody 1978, pp. 306–12; Weisberg and Grofman 1979).

Empirical research is equally unkind to the notion that loss of faith in the system is responsible for declining turnout. Americans who say they are suspicious of politicians and the government vote at the same rate as those who express trust in the political system and the intentions of politicians (Citrin 1978).

2. Data on turnout come from replies to this question: "This month we have some questions about whether people voted in the November 7th Presidential Election. Did (you) (this person) vote in the election held on November 7th?" For almost half the sample, turnout data were provided by the respondent for another member of the household. Such second-hand reporting raises the possibility of misreporting, as Tufte (1977) suggests. This fear seems unjustified, however. Respondents who reported their own vote had a turnout rate of 66.7 percent. People in the sample for whom voting was reported by another household member had a turnout rate of 67.7 percent. We also estimated the effect of secondhand reporting by entering a dummy variable (1 = secondhand reporting) in the probit equation summarized in appendix C. The resulting estimate was −.004, with a standard error of .036. This number is substantially zero, and no change occurred in the coefficients reported in equation 1. Using a different subsample and fewer variables, the estimate reported in Rosenstone and Wolfinger (1978, note 20) was .007,

with a standard error of .010. Although the two estimates themselves differ, together they suggest that the true population parameter is centered at zero.

3. A few sparsely populated states do not provide enough respondents for valid estimates of a single state. This was a problem only with respect to North Dakota, which has no voter registration requirement at all. Otherwise, no such state had any interesting, unique characteristic on any of the variables we used in our analysis. Information on sampling error in the census survey and the procedures for adjusting the standard error of the estimates for groups of states below the regional level can be found in U.S. Bureau of the Census (1975), appendix A, pp. 13–45, 62–66; and U.S. Bureau of the Census (1973b), pp. 13–16.

4. In addition to respondents in these twelve states, we identified some other respondents' state of residence through codes for the largest Standard Metropolitan Statistical Areas (SMSA). Between the state and SMSA codes, we were able to identify the states of more than two-thirds of the 1974 respondents. For the remaining respondents, we coded the registration requirement as the weighted average of the laws in the group of states in their subregional grouping.

5. Using the entire sample would have required fifty *minutes* of computer time for each probit equation estimated. Doubling our subsample would have increased the efficiency of our estimates by only 40 percent, yielding little for the extra expense.

6. Respondents from the District of Columbia were deleted from the subsample and were thus excluded when making the probit estimates. Since their franchise is limited and a great many of District residents maintain legal voting residences elsewhere, we thought we would avoid unnecessary complications. In addition, cases for which data were missing on the income variable were also deleted from the subsample. For these reasons and because the subsampling procedure was random, the number of cases in the subsample is not 10 percent of the actual respondents in the full sample.

7. See Theil (1971), chapter 8. While the case weight provided by the Census Bureau should be applied for descriptive purposes (for example, cross-tabulations), it is not appropriate to apply it for purposes of estimation. See Koch, Freeman, and Freeman (1975) and Porter (1973).

8. The number of cases is not 10 percent of the full sample for the reasons given in footnote 6.

9. In addition, two other variables were deleted from equation 1. The possibility of absentee registration and the hours the polls were open on

election day have a small impact on the probability of voting. In this subsample the estimates for these two variables in equation 1 would have decreased the efficiency of the estimates for the other variables, and they were therefore deleted. Because of the subsampling procedures employed, more efficient estimates for these variables and the other registration provisions are provided by equation 2. See chapter 4 and appendix F.

Chapter 2

1. We tested a number of functional forms to estimate education in the probit analysis. The square of education best fit the data.

2. After testing several functional forms of income, we concluded that the ordinary linear term best fit the data. It should be noted that the categories of the income variable provided by the Bureau of the Census resemble a log scale and are not linear increments of income (see appendix B). Thus although the functional form actually entered in equation 1 is linear, it is linear for the coding categories, which themselves are closer to the log of income.

3. For the preliminary analysis, dummy variables were estimated for each of the occupational groups listed in table 2.3. (The excluded category was people not in the labor force.) Two groups—skilled workers and semiskilled and unskilled workers—had coefficients that could safely be interpreted as zero. These groups became part of the "omitted" category, and estimates were made for the remaining occupational groups.

The estimates for managers and administrators and for farm workers have rather large standard errors. Because the estimates themselves are substantively different from zero, we chose to report the coefficients and note the standard errors rather than delete variables from the equation, which would have treated the coefficients as zero.

4. When operationalizing unemployment, we combined respondents classified as full-time unemployed and men under the age of sixty-five who were not in the labor force. This estimate was made with the control for income removed. Since income is consequent to employment, retaining the control would have led to an underestimation of the effect of unemployment. With this modification, equation 1 was used to estimate the difference in turnout between the unemployed and those who were working. The effect of being unemployed—the difference between the two probit coefficients—was −.071.

5. This distinction may, however, be germane to a group that, to our knowledge, has never before been mentioned in published discussions of political behavior: the 4 percent of the voting-age population who live in mobile homes. They are slightly older and less educated than the rest of the population and include more blue-collar workers. When these and other demographic and contextual variables are held constant, they are still about 8 percent less likely to vote than other citizens. What is more, the effect on voting of living in a trailer persists even for those who have lived in the same spot for at least ten years.

Trailer parks are unpopular with municipal officials and are often consigned to more or less isolated sites on the edge of town or to unincorporated areas. They are surely more conveniently located than most farms, however. Metaphorical remoteness may be more important in explaining trailer dwellers' low turnout, as suggested by one study of a park near the center of a suburban city (Johnson 1971). Factors that evidently are common to many trailer parks strengthened the residents' attachments to "Idle Haven" and weakened their identifications with the larger society. The park provided a rich variety of social and recreational activities. The management was responsible for some services, such as streets and a swimming pool, that are ordinarily provided by local government. Trailer dwellers everywhere seldom own their sites but lease them from the property owner. Thus the residents have no financial stake other than, at most, their trailer. Trailers are not real but personal property and are therefore often taxed at a lower rate than other dwelling units. We conclude that trailer residents, because of emotional separation from the larger community, are less likely to be interested in politics.

6. Both Campbell and his associates (1960, p. 405n) and Lewis-Beck (1977, p. 545n) include in their analysis of farm voting anyone living in a household headed by a farmer. The former also show that their findings would not be altered if they were to exclude farm housewives, as we do (Campbell et al. 1960, p. 407n).

7. This statement is typical of the chapter's conclusions: "In every instance his [the farmer's] participation is substantially less than that of urban blue-collar workers taken as a whole" (Campbell et al. 1960, p. 427). The lower political involvement of farmers is a major theme of what for many years was the most authoritative treatment of "agrarian political behavior." Doubtless this is a source that most political scientists would mention when asked about farmers' voting rates. *But there are no data on turnout in this chapter.* The closest approach is a discussion of

"turnout variability"—represented by people who said they voted in some but not all past presidential elections. Farmers were 7 percentage points more likely than people in urban occupations to give this answer. In fact, as Lewis-Beck showed (1977, p. 550), farmers' turnout in 1952 was only slightly below that of blue-collar workers and was substantially higher in every subsequent year.

8. Another consideration, which Lewis-Beck did not explore, is the changing racial and regional composition of the farm population since the early 1950s. In that era there were millions of Southern subsistence farmers who were unlikely to vote if they were white and were unable to do so if they were black. Since then, the Southern farm population has become whiter, impediments to black voting in the South have been eliminated, and the regional turnout gap has narrowed.

9. Both of these surprising findings are confirmed by a completely different source, an annual study by the Department of Agriculture. In 1975, just 11 percent of all farm workers aged fourteen and over were of Spanish origin, and only 7 percent of hired farmhands were migratory (U.S. Bureau of the Census 1977, p. 691).

Chapter 3

1. We drew the lines in figures 3.1 and 3.2 by plotting turnout for each year of age. The age categories used in figure 3.1 and elsewhere are based on the apparent cutting points in year-by-year turnout. Our large sample enabled us to make more detailed classifications of the elderly, instead of putting everyone more than fifty-four or sixty-four years old in a single category, as is commonly done in research based on ordinary samples.

2. We limit the "married" category to those who are living with their spouses and describe as "unmarried" people who are widowed or divorced, those who never married, and also the 3 percent of our sample who are married but are not living with their spouses.

3. This was estimated by taking the weighted average of the percentage differences between the turnout of men and women over age fifty-four in each of the education and region categories in table 17.11 of Campbell et al. (1960).

4. The probit estimate is −.019, and the standard error is .075. Since working women have much less free time than housewives but have the same voting rate, this finding is also another nail in the coffin of the

proposition that people with more time on their hands are more likely to vote.

5. Because changes in marital status and in the impact of marital status are a function of age, the estimates are comparisons to the turnout of fifty-five-year-olds, taking into consideration both their age and marital status.

6. It might be thought that the estimates displayed in figure 3.4 exaggerate the continued increase in turnout for those over sixty-five because most people of this age are out of the labor force and earn much less than when they were employed. Thus controlling for income, occupation, and ability to work might artificially inflate the turnout of the elderly. Accordingly, we also estimated the effect of age after removing the controls for these three variables. This only slightly reduced the turnout for the oldest age groups, indicating that the central finding still stands: aging itself does not reduce turnout. Consistent with this is the finding that other things being equal, retired men are not less likely to vote than the rest of the population. (We operationalized retirement by a dummy variable for men over age sixty-five who were not in the labor force. The probit estimate is .007; the standard error is .122.)

7. Prior to the enactment of the Twenty-sixth Amendment, people under twenty-one could vote in a few states. Therefore we did not delete from the sample citizens eighteen to twenty years old in Georgia and Kentucky, nineteen and twenty years old in Alaska, and twenty years old in Hawaii.

Chapter 4

1. This aspect of the American electoral system is unusual. In most democratic countries the government assumes responsibility for enrolling all citizens on a permanent, nationwide electoral register. This difference is widely considered a major cause of the low voting rate in the United States.

In 1972, registration was not required in North Dakota and in the more sparsely populated counties of Iowa, Minnesota, Missouri, Ohio, and Wisconsin. By 1976, four states permitted qualified residents to register on election day.

2. Previous research provided reasons for believing that state registration laws had some effect on turnout in the 1952, 1956, and 1960 elections (Campbell et al. 1960, pp. 277–80; Kelley, Ayres, and Bowen 1967; Kim et al. 1975). These studies did not, however, shed much light on

what provisions had *how much* effect on *what kinds of people*. Their contemporary relevance is substantially reduced by the sweeping changes in election laws since 1960.

3. Speeches by a number of advocates of postcard registration can be found in the *Congressional Record*, March 13, 1975, pp. S6450–54.

4. Other sources of controversy were constitutional doubts about expanding the federal role in establishing voter qualifications (a power left to the states by the Constitution), fears about election fraud, and worry about the partisan or ideological advantage that might result from an expanded electorate.

5. The question asked by the Census Bureau in 1966 gave respondents a powerful nudge:

> Two specific reasons were mentioned in the question as it was read by the interviewer, i.e., that the respondent was not a citizen or had not met the local or State residence requirements. In addition, the respondent was invited to give another reason if neither of these adequately explained his failure to register [U.S. Bureau of the Census 1968, p. 3].

This is not, of course, an example of meticulous questionnaire design.

6. Other things being equal, increasing the variance decreases the standard error of the estimate (Finney 1971, pp. 33–37; Theil 1971, pp. 90–91).

7. We excluded respondents in the District of Columbia in order to avoid unnecessary complications that might result because their franchise is limited and many District residents maintain voting addresses elsewhere.

8. Our initial analysis also included these variables: (a) the number of days before the election an absentee ballot had to be obtained; (b) whether the absentee ballot had to be notarized; and (c) whether voting machines were used. These variables had less than 1 percent impact on the probability of voting, and their coefficients were not statistically significant. We deleted them after this early stage of the analysis.

In addition, estimates were made for nonlinear functions of the residency requirement and closing date. This did not appreciably improve the fit. We also estimated interaction terms between each provision and education, between deputy registrars and county registration, and between deputy registrars and irregular office hours. All were insignificant.

Finally, we examined the independent effect on turnout of income and party competition. Poorer people, of course, are less likely to vote, and party competition is often said to result in higher turnout. Thus any estimates of the relationship between registration laws and turnout that omitted consideration of these two variables might lead to a spurious conclusion.

We used the following procedure to determine whether these two variables in the error term should be included in the analysis. For one of these variables to bias the coefficient of a particular registration provision (which we will call X_1), two conditions had to be met. After controlling for the other independent demographic variables, the variable in question had to be correlated both with X_1 and with turnout. If either of these conditions was not met (that is, if one of the partial correlations was zero), then the variable could safely be left out of the analysis without biasing the estimated coefficient for variable X_1.

Using this procedure, we found that income was not correlated with any registration provision, once education, region, and age had been controlled. The average magnitude of the partial correlations of the registration provisions was .029. The partial correlation between competition and turnout was −.009. Therefore, excluding these variables from equation 2 does not bias the estimated coefficients for the registration laws. The measure of party competition we used was adopted from Ranney (1972).

9. This reweighting was accomplished by multiplying, for each case, the original weight by the inverse of the subsampling proportion for the state from which the case was selected. This yields a reweighted N of 126,591. This number is slightly less than the weighted N, mainly because respondents from the District of Columbia were deleted from the probit analysis and, secondarily, because of the random selection of cases in the subsampling procedure.

10. For each respondent, equation 2 was used to compute a probit estimate, which was then converted to a probability by evaluating that number on the cumulative standard normal distribution. The same procedure was followed, altering the values for the variables in equation 2 to simulate changes in the registration provisions. For each respondent these two probabilities were subtracted. The arithmetic mean of these individual probabilities is the estimated aggregate percentage.

11. The standard error of this estimate is 2.1. Thus there is only a 5 percent chance that the true coefficient is less than 4.9 percent or more than 13.3 percent.

12. The one exception is North Dakota, which did not require regis-

tration at all in 1972. Unfortunately, there were not enough respondents from this single state to permit precise estimates of the effects of its unique voting laws.

13. Table 4.2 also shows the effect of liberalized registration laws by income and age. Poorer people would be most affected, as we would expect because of the relationship between education and income. The variation among income categories is much smaller than among people with different educational attainment, however. This reflects the much stronger relationship between education and turnout. Variations by age are small. People in the age groups with the highest turnout would be affected only slightly less than those with the lowest voting rates—citizens under 32 and over 78.

14. For a dissenting view emphasizing "the general insensitivity of partisanship to large changes in turnout," see Converse (1966, p. 29).

15. All the opposition is not based on calculations of partisan or ideological advantage, however. This is particularly true of election day registration plans, which arouse fear of election fraud. A Gallup poll taken during congressional consideration of the Carter plan in 1977 revealed that election day registration was opposed by 67 percent of rank-and-file Republicans and 53 percent of Democrats (*Gallup Opinion Index*, 1977, p. 10).

16. The composition of the actual voters was estimated by using equation 2 to compute a probit estimate for each respondent. The probit estimate was then converted to a probability. The percentage of the voters comprised of people with a given characteristic (for example, a college education) was computed in the following manner:

$$\frac{\sum_{j=1}^{j} \text{probability of voting}}{\sum_{n=1}^{n} \text{probability of voting}} \times 100$$

where j = the number of respondents with a given characteristic (that is, in that category on the variable); and n = the total number of respondents. The same procedure was used to calculate the projected composition of voters, with the values for the registration provisions altered to simulate the liberalized conditions.

We used equation 2 rather than the reported turnout to estimate the composition of the actual voters. If we had used the reported turnout, then the difference between the projected voters and the actual voters would be due both to the simulated changes in registration laws and the residual for each individual in equation 2. These residuals cancel out if equation 2 is used for calculating the composition of both the actual and the projected voters.

17. These projections, as well as those summarized in tables 4.4 and 4.5, are based on the 1972 National Election Study of the University of Michigan Center for Political Studies. For this sample we used equation 2 to estimate both the actual and projected characteristics of voters as described in note 16. We deleted thirteen cases from this sample: the ten respondents from the District of Columbia and three respondents whose education was not reported and for whom turnout therefore could not be predicted. Equation 2 correctly predicted turnout for 74.3 percent of the cases in this sample, as compared with 71.4 percent of the cases in the Current Population Survey subsample. The differences between the actual and projected populations summarized in table 4.3 can be replicated within .4 percentage points by using equation 2 with the Michigan data.

18. In addition, the comparative popularity of Nixon and McGovern, as measured by the proportion of those rating McGovern higher than Nixon on the candidate "feeling thermometers," was identical in the actual and hypothetical voters.

Chapter 5

1. Verba and Nie (1972, p. 170) report that with SES held constant, Northern blacks voted 13 percent more than whites. There are several possible explanations for the difference between their estimate and ours. First, our data were gathered in 1972, theirs in 1967. Second, our subsample has more than three times as many blacks as their sample. Third, they based their estimates on ordinary least squares rather than on probit analysis. Finally, the estimate for race derived by Verba and Nie is probably biased and inconsistent for the following reason. To control for SES, they first regressed turnout on SES and then looked at the relationship between race and the residuals from this equation. This two-step procedure yields biased and inconsistent estimates of the effect of both SES and race. This problem also applies to the other estimates reported by Verba and Nie. See Achen (1977) for a proof of the bias and inconsistency of the estimates produced by this two-step procedure.

2. The findings of higher black turnout may reflect response error. The Michigan 1976 National Election Study ascertained from official

voting records whether each respondent actually voted. False claims of voting by people who had not gone to the polls were distributed fairly evenly among all demographic categories, with one notable exception: black nonvoters were twice as likely as their white counterparts to claim that they had voted (Weisberg 1979).

3. Cuban-Americans are an exception to these generalizations. They are more educated and older and nearly as prosperous as non-Hispanic Americans. They also vote about as much as the rest of the population.

4. Antunes and Gaitz (1975, pp. 1200–02) found that with socio-economic status and age held constant, Chicanos in Houston still voted less than other whites. Our analysis of turnout in 1974 of the 4,637 respondents from Texas (which was self-representing) indicates that with education controlled, Chicanos voted as much as other whites and slightly more than blacks.

5. Turnout in Puerto Rican elections reportedly is 80 percent to 85 percent (Peirce and Hagstrom 1979, p. 551).

6. Some reassurance about our choices came from a Justice Department report on successful prosecutions of state and local officials from 1970 through 1976 (U.S. Department of Justice 1977). Our ten reform states provided a total of nine convicted officials, three each in California, Wisconsin, and North Dakota. Three of our patronage states fared rather well in this scorekeeping. There were no convictions in Rhode Island, two in Indiana, and four in Maryland. The other seven patronage states accounted for a total of 344 convictions. Illinois was in first place, with 139 certifiably corrupt officials, followed by New York with 63, and New Jersey with 56.

7. The probit estimate is .032, with a standard error of .052.

8. The probit estimate is .055, and the standard error is .055.

9. The probit estimate is .072, and the standard error is .299.

Chapter 6

1. This does not necessarily mean that the outcome of any recent presidential election would have been different if the turnout had been higher. Research on the candidate preferences of nonvoters shows no consistent advantage for either party (Reiter 1979; Perry 1973).

REFERENCES

Achen, Christopher H. (1977) "The Bias in 'Normal Vote' Estimates." Department of Political Science, University of California, Berkeley, May.

Aldrich, John, and Cnudde, Charles F. (1975) "Probing the Bounds of Conventional Wisdom: A Comparison of Regression, Probit, and Discriminant Analysis." *American Journal of Political Science* 19 (August 1975), pp. 571–608.

Amundsen, Kirsten. (1977) *A New Look at the Silenced Majority*. Englewood Cliffs, N.J.: Prentice-Hall.

Andersen, Kristi. (1975) "Working Women and Political Participation, 1952–1972." *American Journal of Political Science* 19 (August 1975), pp. 439–53.

Andrews, William G. (1966) "American Voting Participation." *Western Political Quarterly* 19 (December 1966), pp. 639–52.

Antunes, George, and Gaitz, Charles M. (1975) "Ethnicity and Participation: A Study of Mexican-Americans, Blacks and Whites." *American Journal of Sociology* 80 (March 1975), pp. 1192–211.

Arseneau, Robert B., and Wolfinger, Raymond E. (1973) "Voting Behavior in Congressional Elections." Paper read at the annual meeting of the American Political Science Association, New Orleans, September 2–5.

Barber, James David. (1969) *Citizen Politics*. Chicago: Markham.

Barnes, Samuel H. (1977) "Some Political Consequences of Involvement in Organizations." Paper read at the annual meeting of the American Political Science Association, Washington, D.C., September 1–4.

Barry, Brian. (1970) *Sociologists, Economists and Democracy*. Chicago: University of Chicago Press.

Bennett, Stephen E., and Klecka, William R. (1970) "Social Status and Political Participation: A Multivariate Analysis of Predictive Power." *Midwest Journal of Political Science* 14 (August 1970), pp. 355–82.

Brody, Richard A. (1978) "The Puzzle of Political Participation in America." In *The New American Political System*, ed. Anthony King. Washington, D.C.: American Enterprise Institute for Public Policy Research.

Burns v. *Fortson*. (1973) 410 U.S. 686.

Campbell, Angus, Converse, Philip E., Miller, Warren E., and Stokes, Donald E. (1960) *The American Voter*. New York: Wiley.

Campbell, Angus, Gurin, Gerald, and Miller, Warren E. (1954) *The Voter Decides*. Evanston, Ill.: Row, Peterson.

Campbell, Angus, and Kahn, Robert L. (1952) *The People Elect a President*. Ann Arbor: University of Michigan Institute for Social Research.

Center for Political Studies. (1973) 1972 National Election Study. Ann Arbor: University of Michigan Center for Political Studies.

————. (1975) 1974 National Election Study. Ann Arbor: University of Michigan Center for Political Studies.

————. (1977) 1976 National Election Study. Ann Arbor: University of Michigan Center for Political Studies.

Citrin, Jack. (1978) "The Alienated Voter." *Taxing and Spending*, October 1978, pp. 1–7.

Clausen, Aage R. (1969) "Response Validity in Surveys." *Public Opinion Quarterly* 32 (Winter 1968–69), pp. 588–606.

Congressional Quarterly Weekly Report, May 14, 1977, pp. 909–11.

Converse, Philip E. (1966) "The Concept of a Normal Vote." In *Elections and the Political Order*, ed. Angus Campbell et al., pp. 9–39. New York: Wiley.

————. (1976) *The Dynamics of Party Support*. Beverly Hills, Calif.: Sage.

Converse, Philip E., with Niemi, Richard. (1971) "Non-voting among Young Adults in the United States." In *Political Parties and Political Behavior*, ed. William J. Crotty et al. 2nd ed. Boston: Allyn and Bacon.

Cox, D. R. (1970) *The Analysis of Binary Data*. London: Methuen.

Cutler, Neal E. (1977) "Demographic, Social-Psychological, and Political Factors in the Politics of Aging: A Foundation for Research in 'Political Gerontology.' " *American Political Science Review* 71 (September 1977), pp. 1011–25.

Dahl, Robert A. (1961) *Who Governs?* New Haven, Conn.: Yale University Press.

Dawson, Richard E. (1973). *Public Opinion and Contemporary Disarray*. New York: Harper and Row.

Downs, Anthony. (1957) *An Economic Theory of Democracy*. New York: Harper and Row.

Dunn v. *Blumstein*. (1972) 405 U.S. 330.

Dye, Thomas R. (1966) *Politics, Economics, and the Public.* Chicago: Rand McNally.

Elazar, Daniel J. (1972) *American Federalism: A View from the States.* 2nd ed. New York: Thomas Y. Crowell.

Erikson, Robert S. (1979) "Why Do People Vote? Because They Are Registered." Paper read at the National Science Foundation Conference on Voter Turnout, San Diego, May 16–19.

Ferejohn, John A., and Fiorina, Morris P. (1979) "The Decline in Turnout in Presidential Elections." Paper read at the National Science Foundation Conference on Voter Turnout, San Diego, May 16–19.

Finney, D. J. (1971) *Probit Analysis.* 3rd ed. Cambridge: Cambridge University Press.

Flanigan, William H., and Zingale, Nancy H. (1975) *Political Behavior of the American Electorate.* 3rd ed. Boston: Allyn and Bacon.

Frey, Bruno S. (1971) "Why do High Income People Participate More in Politics?" *Public Choice*, Fall 1971, pp. 101–05.

———. (1972) "Reply." *Public Choice*, Fall 1972, pp. 119–22.

Glaser, William A. (1959) "The Family and Voting Turnout." *Public Opinion Quarterly* 23 (Winter 1959), pp. 563–70.

Glenn, Norval D., and Grimes, Michael. (1968) "Aging, Voting, and Political Interest." *American Sociological Review* 33 (August 1968), pp. 563–75.

Goldberger, Arthur S. (1964) *Econometric Theory.* New York: Wiley.

Hanushek, Eric A., and Jackson, John E. (1977) *Statistical Methods for Social Scientists.* New York: Academic Press.

Harper v. Virginia State Board of Elections. (1966) 383 U.S. 663.

Hout, Michael and Knoke, David (1975) "Change in Voting Turnout, 1952–1972." *Public Opinion Quarterly* 39 (Spring 1975), pp. 52–68.

ISR Newsletter. (1977) Ann Arbor: University of Michigan Institute for Social Research, Summer, p. 3.

Johnson, Charles A. (1976) "Political Culture in American States: Elazar's Formulation Examined." *American Journal of Political Science*, August 1976, pp. 491–509.

Johnson, Sheila K. (1971) *Idle Haven: Community Building among the Working-Class Retired.* Berkeley: University of California Press.

Johnston, J. (1972) *Econometric Methods.* 2nd ed. New York: McGraw-Hill.

Kelley, Jr., Stanley, Ayres, Richard E., and Bowen, William G. (1967) "Registration and Voting: Putting First Things First." *American Polit-*

ical Science Review 61 (June 1967), pp. 359–79.

Kennedy, Edward M. (1975) Remarks in the *Congressional Record,* March 13, 1975, pp. S6450–54.

Key, Jr., V. O. (1964) *Politics, Parties, and Pressure Groups.* 5th ed. New York: Thomas Y. Crowell.

Kim, Jae-On, Petrocik, John R., and Enokson, Stephen N. (1975) "Voter Turnout Among the American States: Systemic and Individual Components." *American Political Science Review* 69 (March 1975), pp. 107–123.

Koch, Gary G., Freeman, Jr., Daniel H., and Freeman, Jean L. (1975) "Strategies in the Multivariate Analysis of Data from Complex Surveys." *International Statistical Review,* January 1975, pp. 59–78.

Kraut, R. E., and McConahay, J. B. (1973) "How Being Interviewed Affects Voting: An Experiment." *Public Opinion Quarterly* 37 (Fall 1973), pp. 393–406.

Lane, Robert E. (1959) *Political Life.* New York: Free Press of Glencoe.

League of Women Voters Education Fund. (1972) *Registration and Absentee Voting Procedures by State, 1972.* Washington, D.C.: League of Women Voters.

Lewis-Beck, Michael S. (1977) "Agrarian Political Behavior in the United States." *American Journal of Political Science,* 21 (August 1977) pp. 543–65.

Library of Congress, Congressional Research Service. (1972) *Election Laws of The Fifty States and the District of Columbia* (April.) Washington, D.C.: Library of Congress.

Lipset, Seymour Martin. (1960) *Political Man.* New York: Doubleday.

Marston v. *Lewis.* (1973) 410 U.S. 679.

Matthews, Donald R., and Prothro, James W. (1966) *Negroes and the New Southern Politics.* New York: Harcourt, Brace and World.

McGee, Gale. (1975) Remarks in the *Congressional Record,* March 13, 1975, p. S6451.

Meehl, Paul E. (1977) "The Selfish Voter Paradox and the Thrown-Away Vote Argument." *American Political Science Review,* 71 (March 1977), pp. 11–30.

Milbrath, Lester W. (1965) *Political Participation.* Chicago: Rand McNally.

———. (1971) "Individuals and Government." In *Politics in the American States,* ed. Herbert Jacob and Kenneth N. Vines. 2nd ed. Boston: Little, Brown.

Milbrath, Lester W., and Goel, M. L. (1977) *Political Participation*. 2nd ed. Chicago: Rand McNally.

New York Times. (1979) February 18, 1972, p. 16.

Nie, Norman H., Powell, G. Bingham, and Prewitt, Kenneth. (1969) "Social Structure and Political Participation." *American Political Science Review*, 62 (June and September 1969), pp. 361–78, 808–32.

Niemi, Richard G., Hedges, Roman, and Jennings, M. Kent. (1977) "The Similarity of Husbands' and Wives' Political Views." *American Politics Quarterly* 5 (April 1977), pp. 133–48.

Olsen, Marvin E. (1970) "Social and Political Participation of Blacks." *American Sociological Review* 35 (August 1970), pp. 682–97.

O'Rourke, Timothy G. (1978) "Communication." *American Political Science Review* 72 (December 1978), pp. 1360–61.

Peirce, Neal R., and Hagstrom, Jerry. (1979) "The Hispanic Community —A Growing Force to be Reckoned With." *National Journal*, April 7, 1979, pp. 548–55.

Perry, Paul (1973). "A Comparison of the Voting Preferences of Likely Voters and Likely Nonvoters." *Public Opinion Quarterly* 37 (Spring 1973), pp. 99–109.

Phillips, Kevin P., and Blackman, Paul H. (1975) *Electoral Reform and Voter Participation*. Washington, D.C.: American Enterprise Institute for Public Policy Research.

Pindyck, Robert S., and Rubinfeld, Daniel L. (1976) *Economic Models and Economic Forecasts*. New York: McGraw-Hill.

Pitkin, Hanna F. (1967) *The Concept of Representation*. Berkeley: University of California Press.

Polsby, Nelson W., and Wildavsky, Aaron. (1976) *Presidential Elections*. 4th ed. New York: Scribner's.

Porter, Richard D. (1973) "On the Use of Survey Sample Weights in the Linear Model." *Annals of Economic and Social Measurement*, June 1973, pp. 74–75.

Ranney, Austin. (1972) "Parties in State Politics." In *Politics in the American States*, ed. Herbert Jacob and Kenneth N. Vines. 2nd ed. Boston: Little, Brown.

Reiter, Howard L. (1979) "Why is Turnout Down?" *Public Opinion Quarterly* 43 (Fall 1979), pp. 297–311.

Reitman, Alan, and Davidson, Robert B. (1972) *The Election Process: Voting Laws and Procedures*. Dobbs Ferry, N.Y.: Oceana.

Riker, William H., and Ordeshook, Peter C. (1973) *An Introduction to*

Positive Political Theory. Englewood Cliffs, N.J.: Prentice-Hall.

Robinson, John P., and Converse, Philip E. (1972) "Social Change in the Use of Time." In *The Human Meaning of Social Change*, ed. Angus Campbell and Philip E. Converse, pp. 74–75. New York: Russell Sage Foundation.

Roper, Elmo. (1961) "How to Lose Your Vote." *Saturday Review*, March 18, 1961, pp. 14–15.

Rosenstone, Steven J., and Wolfinger, Raymond E. (1978) "The Effect of Registration Laws on Voter Turnout." *American Political Science Review* 72 (March 1978), pp. 22–45.

Rosenstone, Steven J., Wolfinger, Raymond E., and McIntosh, Richard A. (1978) "Voter Turnout in Midterm Elections." Paper read at the annual meeting of the Americal Political Science Association, New York, August 31–September 3.

San Francisco Chronicle. (1977) May 9, p. 8; May 16, p. 38; July 27, p. 1.

Sharkansky, Ira. (1969) "The Utility of Elazar's Political Culture: A Research Note." *Polity*, Fall 1969, pp. 247–62.

Sniderman, Paul M. (1975) *Personality and Democratic Politics*. Berkeley: University of California Press.

Stafford, Frank, and Duncan, Greg. (1977) "The Use of Time and Technology in the United States." Department of Economics, University of Michigan, July.

Sterling, Carleton W. (1979) "Communication." *American Political Science Review* 73 (June 1979), pp. 539–42.

Tarrance, V. Lance. (1976) "The Vanishing Voter: A Look at Non-Voting as a Purposive Act." In *Voters, Primaries and Parties*, ed. Jonathan Moore and Albert C. Pierce. Cambridge, Mass.: Harvard University Institute of Politics.

Theil, Henri. (1971) *Principles of Econometrics*. New York: Wiley.

Thornton, Robert. (1972) "Election Legislation." In *The Book of the States, 1972–1973*, pp. 25–30. Lexington, Ky.: Council of State Governments.

Tolchin, Martin, and Tolchin, Susan. (1972) *To the Victor . . .* New York: Random House.

Traugott, Michael W., and Katosh, John P. (1979) "Response Validity in Surveys of Voting Behavior." *Public Opinion Quarterly* 43 (Fall 1979), pp. 359–77.

Tufte, Edward R. (1977) "Political Statistics for the United States: Observations on Some Major Data Sources." *American Political Science Review* 71 (March 1977), pp. 305–14.

U.S. Bureau of the Census. (1963) *Current Population Survey: A Report on Methodology.* U.S. Department of Commerce technical paper no. 7.

———. (1968) "Voting and Registration in the Election of November 1966." In *Current Population Reports, Population Characteristics.* U.S. Department of Commerce series P-20, no. 174.

———. (1972) "Projections of the Population of Voting Age for States: November 1972." In *Current Population Reports, Population Characteristics.* U.S. Department of Commerce series P-25, no. 479.

———. (1973a) *Public Employment in 1972.* U.S. Department of Commerce annual publication, Table 8.

———. (1973b) "Voting and Registration in the Election of November 1972." In *Current Population Reports, Population Characteristics.* U.S. Department of Commerce series P-20, no. 253.

———. (1973c) *Statistical Abstract of the United States: 1973.* Washington, D.C.: U.S. Government Printing Office.

———. (1975) "Documentation of the Annual Demographic File." U.S. Department of Commerce mimeographed document, appendix A.

———. (1976a) "Voting and Registration in the Election of November 1974," *Current Population Reports, Population Characteristics.* U.S. Department of Commerce series P-20, no. 293.

———. (1976b) *Statistical Abstract of the United States: 1976.* Washington, D.C.: U.S. Government Printing Office.

———. (1977) *Statistical Abstract of the United States: 1977.* Washington, D.C.: U.S. Government Printing Office.

———. (1978) *Current Population Survey: Design and Methodology.* U.S. Department of Commerce technical paper no. 40.

U.S. Department of Justice, Criminal Division, Public Integrity Section. (1977) "Federal Prosecutions of Corrupt Public Officials 1970–1976." February 8.

U.S. Senate, Committee on Post Office and Civil Service. (1972) "Proposed Federal Registration of Voters—How the States Now Provide for Voter Registration," *Congressional Record,* March 8, 1972, pp. 7530–31.

Verba, Sidney, and Nie, Norman H. (1972) *Participation in America.* New York: Harper and Row.

Verba, Sidney, Nie, Norman H., and Kim, Jae-on. (1978) *Participation and Political Equality*. New York: Cambridge University Press.

Weisberg, Herbert F. (1979) "The Validity of Voter Registration and Turnout Reports in Surveys." Paper read at the National Science Foundation Conference on Voter Turnout, May 16–19, San Diego.

Weisberg, Herbert F., and Grofman, Bernard. (1979) "Candidate Evaluations and Turnout." Paper read at the National Science Foundation Conference on Voter Turnout, San Diego, May 16–19.

Whyte, William F. (1955) *Street Corner Society*. Enlarged ed. Chicago: University of Chicago Press.

Wolfinger, Raymond E. (1974) *The Politics of Progress*. Englewood Cliffs, N.J.: Prentice-Hall.

Wolfinger, Raymond E., and Arseneau, Robert B. (1978) "Partisan Change in the South, 1952–1976." In *Political Parties: Development and Decay*, ed. Louis Maisel and Joseph Cooper, pp. 179–210. Beverly Hills, Calif.: Sage.

Yalch, Richard F. (1976) "Pre-Election Interview Effects on Voter Turnout." *Public Opinion Quarterly* 40 (Fall 1976), pp. 331–36.

Zitter, Meyer, and Starsinic, Donald E. (1966) "Estimates of 'Eligible' Voters in Small Areas; Some First Approximations." *Proceedings of the Social Statistics Section of the American Statistical Association*, pp. 368–78.

INDEX

DAVID

OB1